The Thousand Year War
in the Mideast

Depicted above and on the front cover:
Vought F8U-1 Crusader
in the markings of VF-211, USS Hancock 1960

(The author selected this jet fighter.
Read page 116 of this book for further background.)

Maps

I have ever deemed it fundamental for the United States never to take active part in the quarrels of Europe. Their political interests are entirely distinct from ours. Their mutual jealousies, their balance of power, their complicated alliances, their forms and principles of government, are all foreign to us. They are nations of eternal war."

— Thomas Jefferson, 1823

..."a passionate attachment of one nation for another produces a variety of evils. Sympathy for the favorite nation, facilitating the illusion of an imaginary common interest in cases where no real common interest exists, and infusing into one the enmities of the other, betrays the former into a participation in the quarrels and wars of the latter, without adequate inducement or justification. It leads also to concession to the favorite nation of privileges denied to others, which is apt doubly to injure the nation making the concessions; by unnecessarily parting with what ought to have been retained; and by exciting jealousy, ill-will and a disposition to retaliate, in the parties from whom equal privileges are withheld. And it gives to ambitious, corrupted or deluded citizens (who devote themselves to the favorite nation) facility to betray, or sacrifice the interests of their own country, without odium, sometimes even with popularity .... Against the insidious wiles of foreign influence, (I conjure you to believe me fellow-citizen) the jealousy of a free people ought to be constantly awake."

— George Washington
FAREWELL ADDRESS, 1796

"Never was so much false arithmetic employed on any subject, as that which has been employed to persuade nations that it is in their interest to go to war."

— Thomas Jefferson, 1782

About the "Uncle Eric" Series

The "Uncle Eric" series of books is written by Richard J. Maybury for young and old alike. Using the epistolary style of writing (using letters to tell a story), Mr. Maybury plays the part of an economist writing a series of letters to his niece or nephew. Using stories and examples, he gives interesting and clear explanations of topics that are generally thought to be too difficult for anyone but experts.

Mr. Maybury warns, "beware of anyone who tells you a topic is above you or better left to experts. Many people are twice as smart as they think they are but they've been intimidated into believing some topics are above them. You can understand almost anything if it is explained well."

The series is called UNCLE ERIC'S MODEL OF HOW THE WORLD WORKS (For a full explanation see pages 8-13 of this book). Each book in the series attempts to be consistent with the principles of America's Founders. The books can be read in any order, and have been written to stand alone. To get the most from each one, however, Mr. Maybury suggests the following order of reading.

Uncle Eric's Model
of How the World Works

Uncle Eric Talks About Personal, Career and Financial Security

Whatever Happened to Penny Candy?

Whatever Happened to Justice?

Are You Liberal? Conservative? or Confused?

Ancient Rome: How It Affects You Today

Evaluating Books: What Would Thomas Jefferson Think About This?

The Money Mystery

The Clipper Ship Strategy

The Thousand Year War in the Mideast: How It Affects You Today

World War II: How It Affects You Today (future title)

(Study guides available or forthcoming for above titles.)

An "Uncle Eric Book"

The Thousand Year War
in the Mideast

How It Affects You Today

Sequel to ANCIENT ROME: HOW IT AFFECTS YOU TODAY

by Richard J. Maybury
("Uncle Eric")

published by
Bluestocking Press
P.O. Box 1014 • Dept. TYW
Placerville • CA • 95667-1014

Printed and bound in the United States of America.

Cover illustration by Bob O'Hara, Georgetown, CA
Castle illustration (page 72) by Bob O'Hara, Georgetown, CA
Jet fighter illustration (page 116) by Bob O'Hara, Georgetown, CA

Edited by Jane A. Williams

Library of Congress Cataloging-in-Publication Data
Maybury, Rick.
    The thousand year war in the Mideast : how it affects you today / by Richard J. Maybury (Uncle Eric).
        p. cm. -- (An "Uncle Eric" book)
    Includes bibliographical references (p.   ) and index.
    ISBN 0-942617-32-0 (alk. paper)
    1. Rome--Politics and government--30 B.C. 476 A.D. 2. World politics--20th century. 3. Civilization, Modern--Roman influences. 4. Middle East--History. I. Title. II. Series: Maybury, Rick. "Uncle Eric" book.
DG273.M39   1999
909.82--dc21   99-11076
                                                            CIP

Published by
Bluestocking Press
Post Office Box 1014, Dept. TYW, Placerville, CA 95667-1014

To my father,
who taught me to always
try to see it from the other person's point of view.

Uncle Eric's Model
of How the World Works

What is a model? In his book UNCLE ERIC TALKS ABOUT PERSONAL, CAREER AND FINANCIAL SECURITY, Richard Maybury (Uncle Eric) explains that one of the most important things you can teach children, or learn yourself, is:

"Models are how we think, they are how we understand how the world works. As we go through life we build these very complex pictures in our minds of how the world works, and we're constantly referring back to them — matching incoming data against our models. That's how we make sense of things. One of the most important uses for models is in sorting incoming information to decide if it's important or not.

"In most schools, models are never mentioned because the teachers are unaware of them. One of the most dangerous weaknesses in traditional education is that it contains no model for political history. Teachers teach what they were taught — and no one ever mentioned models to them, so they don't teach them to their students. For the most part, children are just loaded down with collections of facts that they are made to memorize. Without good models, children have no way to know which facts are important and which are not. Students leave school thinking history is a senseless waste of time. Then, deprived of the real lessons of history, the student is vulnerable."

The question is, which models to teach. Mr. Maybury says, "the two models that I think are crucially important for everyone to learn are economics and law."

WHATEVER HAPPENED TO PENNY CANDY? explains the economic model, which is based on Austrian economics, the most free-market of all economic models. WHATEVER HAPPENED TO JUSTICE? explains the legal model, and shows the connection between rational law and economic progress. The legal model is the old British Common Law — or Natural Law. The original principles on which America was founded were those of the old British Common Law.

These two books, PENNY CANDY and JUSTICE, provide the overall model of how human civilization works, especially the world of money.

Once the model is understood, read ARE YOU LIBERAL? CONSERVATIVE? OR CONFUSED? which explains political philosophies relative to Uncle Eric's Model — and makes a strong case for consistency to that model, no exceptions.

Next, read ANCIENT ROME: HOW IT AFFECTS YOU TODAY which shows what happens when a society ignores Uncle Eric's Model and embraces fascism.

To help you locate books and authors generally in agreement with these economic and legal models, Mr. Maybury wrote EVALUATING BOOKS: WHAT WOULD THOMAS JEFFERSON THINK ABOUT THIS? which provides guidelines for selecting books that are consistent with the principles of America's founders. You can apply these guidelines to books, movies, news commentators, current events — to any spoken or written medium.

Further expanding on the economic model is THE MONEY MYSTERY which explains the hidden force affecting your career, business and investments. Some economists refer to this force as velocity, others to money demand. Whichever term is used, it is one of the least understood forces affecting your life. Knowing about velocity and money demand not only gives you an understanding of history that few others have, it prepares you to understand and avoid pitfalls in your career, business and investments. THE MONEY MYSTERY is the first sequel to WHATEVER HAPPENED TO PENNY CANDY? Essential background for getting the most from CLIPPER SHIP STRATEGY.

THE CLIPPER SHIP STRATEGY explains how government's interference in the economy affects business, careers and investments. It's a practical nuts-and-bolts strategy for prospering in our turbulent economy. This book is the second sequel to WHATEVER HAPPENED TO PENNY CANDY? and should be read after THE MONEY MYSTERY.

THE THOUSAND YEAR WAR IN THE MIDEAST: HOW IT AFFECTS YOU TODAY explains how events on the other side of the world a thousand years ago can affect us more than events in our own hometowns today. In the 1970s, '80s and '90s, the Thousand Year War has been the cause of great shocks to the investment markets — the oil embargoes, the Iranian hostage crisis, the Iraq-Kuwait war, and the Caucasus Wars over the Caspian Sea oil basin — and it is likely to remain so for decades to come. Forewarned is forearmed. You must understand where this war is leading to manage your career, business and investments.

The economic crisis and turmoil in the stock market that began in 1997 affects our daily lives profoundly, and probably will continue to do so for years to come. This disturbance had its origin in foreign nations — nations in which the U.S. government intervenes on a regular basis. The justification for these interventions grew out of the Hollywood movie view of World War II. How accurate is this view? In his forthcoming book, WORLD WAR II: HOW IT AFFECTS YOU TODAY, Richard Maybury (Uncle Eric) gives the other side of the story, the side you are not likely to get anywhere else.

These books can be read in any order and have been written to stand alone. But to get the most from each one, Mr. Maybury suggests the following order of reading:

Uncle Eric's Model
of How the World Works

Book 1.   UNCLE ERIC TALKS ABOUT PERSONAL, CAREER AND FINANCIAL SECURITY.
Uncle Eric's Model introduced. For a civilization to have the most individual liberty and the most prosperity it must have a free market economic system, as well as a legal system based on higher law principles.

Book 2.   WHATEVER HAPPENED TO PENNY CANDY? *A Fast, Clear and Fun Explanation of the Economics You Need for Success in Your Career, Business and Investments.*
The economic model explained. The clearest most interesting explanation of economics around. *(Study Guide available.)*

Book 3.   WHATEVER HAPPENED TO JUSTICE?
The legal model explained. Explores America's legal heritage. Discusses the difference between higher law and man-made law, and the connection between rational law and economic prosperity.

Book 4.   ARE YOU LIBERAL? CONSERVATIVE? OR CONFUSED?
Political labels. What do they mean? Liberal, conservative, left, right, democrat, republican, moderate, socialist, libertarian, communist—what

are their economic policies and what plans do their promoters have for your money? Clear, concise explanations. Facts and fallacies. The model applied and misapplied.

Book 5.   ANCIENT ROME: *How It Affects You Today.*
The model ignored. Are we heading for fascism like ancient Rome? Mr. Maybury uses historical events to explain current events. Take a look at ancient Roman government and how it affects you today.
(Study Guide available.)

Book 6.   EVALUATING BOOKS: *What Would Thomas Jefferson Think About This?*
Learn how to identify the philosophical slant of most writers and media commentators on the subjects of law, history, economics, and literature.

Book 7.   THE MONEY MYSTERY: *The Hidden Force Affecting Your Career, Business and Investments.* Some economists refer to velocity, others to money demand. However it is seen, it is one of the least understood forces affecting our businesses, careers and investments. The first sequel to WHATEVER HAPPENED TO PENNY CANDY?, THE MONEY MYSTERY prepares you to understand and avoid pitfalls in your career, business and investments.

Book 8.   THE CLIPPER SHIP STRATEGY: *For Success in Your Career, Business and Investments.* Practical nuts-and-bolts strategy for prospering in our turbulent economy, CLIPPER SHIP STRATEGY is the second sequel to WHATEVER HAPPENED TO PENNY CANDY? and should be read after THE MONEY MYSTERY.

Book 9:   THE THOUSAND YEAR WAR IN THE MIDEAST: *How It Affects You Today.* Events on the other side of the world a thousand years ago can affect us more than events in our hometowns today. In the 1970s, '80s and '90s, the Thousand Year War has been the cause of great shocks to the economy and investment markets, including the oil embargoes, the Iranian hostage crisis, the Iraq-Kuwait war, and the Caucasus Wars over the Caspian Sea oil basin among others — and it is likely to remain so for decades to come. Forewarned is forearmed. To successfully manage your career, business and investments you must understand this war.

Book 10: WORLD WAR II: *How It Affects You Today.* The economic crisis and turmoil in the stock market that began in 1997 affects our daily lives profoundly, and probably will continue to do so for years to come. This disturbance had its origin in foreign nations — nations in which the U.S. government intervenes on a regular basis. The justification for these interventions grew out of the Hollywood movie view of World War II. How accurate is this view? Richard Maybury (Uncle Eric) gives the other side of the story, the side you are not likely to get anywhere else. *Future title.*

Study Guides
are available or forthcoming
for the "Uncle Eric" books.

Quantity Discounts Available

This book, and all other books in the "Uncle Eric" series, are available at special quantity discounts for bulk purchases to individuals, businesses, schools, libraries, and associations, to be distributed as gifts, premiums, or as fund raisers.

For terms and discount schedule contact:

Marketing Department
Bluestocking Press
P.O. Box 1014
Dept. TYW
Placerville, CA 95667-1014
Phone: 800-959-8586; 530-621-1123
Fax: 530-642-9222

Specify how books are to be distributed: as gifts, premiums, fund raisers — or to be resold.

Note to Reader

Throughout the book, when a word that appears in the glossary is introduced in the text, it is displayed in **bold typeface.**

Contents

Author's Disclosure

For reasons I do not understand, writers today are supposed to be objective. Few disclose the viewpoints or opinions they use to decide what information is important and what is not, or what shall be presented or omitted.

I do not adhere to this standard and make no pretense of being objective. I am biased in favor of liberty, free markets and international neutrality, and proud of it. So, I disclose my viewpoint which you will find explained in detail in my newsletter and my other books.[1] My main objective is to give the other side of the story, the non-statist side that has been almost completely erased from the schools, from the news media and from the entertainment media.

For those who have not yet read my newsletter or other books, I call my viewpoint Juris Naturalism (pronounced *jur*-es *nach*-e-re-liz-em, sometimes abbreviated JN) meaning the belief in a natural law that is higher than any government's law. Here are six quotes from America's founders that help describe this viewpoint:

> "...all men are created equal, that they are endowed by their Creator with certain unalienable rights."
> — DECLARATION OF INDEPENDENCE, 1776

> "The natural rights of the colonists are these: first, a right to life; second to liberty; third to property; together with the right to support and defend them in the best manner they can."
> — Samuel Adams, 1772

---

[1] See RICHARD MAYBURY'S EARLY WARNING REPORT newsletter, published by Henry-Madison Research, Box 1616-WY, Rocklin, CA, 95677, and his books (see pgs.11-13), Bluestocking Press, Placerville, CA, 95667.

"It is strangely absurd to suppose that a million of human beings collected together are not under the same moral laws which bind each of them separately."
— Thomas Jefferson, 1816

"A wise and frugal government, which shall restrain men from injuring one another, which shall leave them otherwise free to regulate their own pursuits of industry and improvement, and shall not take from the mouth of labor the bread it has earned. This is the sum of good government."
— Thomas Jefferson, 1801

"Not a place on earth might be so happy as America. Her situation is remote from all the wrangling world, and she has nothing to do but to trade with them."
— Thomas Paine, 1776

"The great rule of conduct for us, in regard to foreign nations, is, in extending our commercial relations, to have with them as little political connection as possible."
— George Washington, 1796

George
Washington

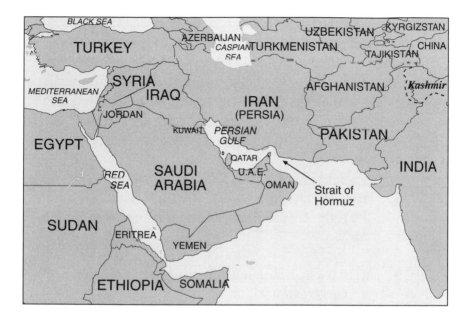

The Middle East, or Mideast is not well defined but is generally taken to be the area from Egypt to Afghanistan, and from Turkey to Yemen. This is where the Thousand Year War began, and it remains the central battlefield today. The Persian Gulf has 65% of the total world oil supply. Most of the oil is held by the U.S.-backed dictatorships on the west side. Evidence indicates the Iraqi and Iranian dictatorships plan to take the gulf back.

On August 2, 1990, Iraqi forces invaded Kuwait. By March 2, 1991, Iraqi forces had been defeated and U.S. officials had announced "it's over."

Anyone who honestly believes the Mideast war is over is not paying attention. The Iraq-Kuwait war was just one in a long string of Mideast conflicts in which America has been involved. Here is a partial list of recent events in or related to the Mideast:

1968   Robert F. Kennedy wishes to supply Israel with F-4 jet fighters. He is killed by Jordanian-born Sirhan Sirhan

1973   U.S. backs Israel in Arab-Israeli war. First Arab oil embargo against U.S.

1979   Iranian hostage crisis. Second major oil crisis.

1981   First Gulf of Sidra incident, two Libyan jets shot down.

1983   241 Marines killed in bombing of barracks in Lebanon.

1986   Achille Lauro Cruise ship hijacked.

1986   U.S. bombing of Tripoli.

1987   U.S. fleet in Persian Gulf, Iraqi missile attack on USS Stark.

1988   Vincenes incident, Iranian jetliner shot down by U.S. warship.

1988   Pan Am Flight 103 blown up over Lockerbie, Scotland, killing 270.

1989   Second Gulf of Sidra incident, two more Libyan jets shot down.

1990   Iraq invades Kuwait, operations Desert Shield and Desert Storm.

1993   Attack at CIA building in Washington, four killed. World Trade Center bombing.[2]

1994   War between Chechens (Moslems) and Russians (Christians). U.S. supplies military training and money to Kremlin.

1996   Khobar Towers bombing in Saudi Arabia, 19 Americans killed.

1997   Arab oil dictators supposedly allied with U.S. begin forming ties with Iran.

1997   Islamic[3] party elected to leadership of Pakistan.

---

[2] Killed 6, injured about 1,000. Total cost, $1,080,000,000; 350 companies and 40,000 workers displaced. Source: Wall Street Journal, December 17, 1997

[3] Moslem

1998   Beginning of nuclear arms race between Pakistan and India.

1998   War between Moslems and Serbs (Christians) in Kosovo.

1998   U.S. war planes still patrolling two no-fly zones over Iraq. U.S. troops still in Balkans. Bombing of two U.S. embassies in Africa, and U.S. retaliatory bombing of Islamic guerrilla training camps in Afghanistan. Subsequent retaliatory bombing of American-franchised Planet Hollywood restaurant in Cape Town, South Africa.

These events are just the tip of the iceberg, and they are only the beginning.

"Terrorists with access to deadly chemical and biological bombs are 'going to change the way in which the American people view security in our own country' said Defense Secretary William S. Cohen."

Army Times, September 22, 1997

The main enemies of the U.S. government are the governments of Iraq, Iran, Sudan, Libya, Syria, China, North
Korea and Serbia. Other likely enemies are the governments of Pakistan, Chechnya and the Taliban in Afghanistan. Have these enemies formed a secret alliance, a New
Axis?

Chaostan

Chaostan

Chaostan (pronunciation: Chaos-tan) is a term coined by Richard Maybury (Uncle Eric) to mean the area from the Arctic Ocean to the Indian Ocean, and Poland to the Pacific, plus North Africa. The name is derived from the fact that in Central Asia the suffix stan means "the land of." Afghanistan is the land of the Afghans, Uzbekistan is the land of the Uzbeks. Chaostan is the land of chaos.

This name was chosen because of the two laws that make civilization possible: (1) do all you have agreed to do and (2) do not encroach on other persons or their property. The first is the basis of contract law, the second is the basis of tort law and some criminal law.

These two laws, common to all religions, are ethical bedrock. They were the basis of the old British Common Law, on which the American founders based the Declaration of Independence, Constitution and Bill of Rights.

Chaostan is the most important area that never developed legal systems based on these two laws.

In the absence of these laws, the only possibilities are tyranny or chaos. Genuine liberty and free markets are not an option.

For centuries, Chaostan has had tyranny. Now the area is deeply into chaos.

Mr. Maybury ("Uncle Eric") believes the available evidence indicates that Chaostan is headed for widespread war, and the war will profoundly affect the economy and our careers, business and investments.

(For more information about Chaostan, see the Appendix.)

1

Terrorism or Retaliation?

"Most of the killing taking place around the world in recent years
has been caused by religious conflict. ... Religious fundamentalism, long
suppressed by the Cold War, [is] now bursting forth in all righteous and
murderous rage."

— Arthur Schlesinger, Jr. WALL STREET JOURNAL, 11/22/95

Dear Chris,

Thanks for your letter and your questions. You mentioned
that in doing research on the Internet for a school paper you
stumbled across a web site that lists terrorist activities against
the U.S. You found it alarming.

You are right to be concerned about terrorist acts inside
the United States. For a long time Americans believed
terrorism was something that happened in other places.

What's changed? Why is the United States being targeted
by terrorists? What's gone wrong? And, why can't the U.S.
government protect us from these "maniacs?"

After all, what have innocent U.S. citizens done to war-
rant retaliation by terrorists?

Do you remember in our prior set of letters on Ancient Rome[4], I said that I am often amazed at how events on the other side of the world a thousand years ago affect us more than events in our hometowns today? They affect us not in a subtle or general way, but very immediately on a day to day basis.

As an example, I mentioned the conflict between the Christian and Moslem worlds that began during the Middle Ages. This letter is the first of a series that will get deeply into that subject.

> "The farther back you can look, the farther forward you are likely to see."
>
> Winston Churchill

That ancient conflict between the Christian and Moslem worlds led to the Iraq-Kuwait war in 1990, which caused 299 American deaths, an estimated 100,000 Iraqi deaths, and caused oil prices to double and the stock market to fall 19%.

Chris, the Iraq-Kuwait war was just one small episode in the thousand year Mideast war. (For a brief history of the Iraq-Kuwait war, see the Appendix.)

"Terrorism" is a part of this war. For centuries, the U.S. was not involved. One reason, obviously, is that the U.S. is a very young country.

Also, until this century, America was neutral and in most cases tried to stay out of the wars of the Old World. Thomas Jefferson referred to Europe as "nations of eternal war," and when we look at the wars in, for instance, the Balkans, it's hard to disagree.

---

[4] Uncle Eric is referring to ANCIENT ROME: HOW IT AFFECTS YOU TODAY by Richard J. Maybury, Bluestocking Press, Placerville, CA, 95667.

The nations of the Balkan Peninsula are Slovenia, Croatia, Bosnia, Yugoslavia (Serbia, Vojvodina, Kosovo and Montenegro), Hungary, Romania, Moldova, Bulgaria, Macedonia, Albania, Greece and the European portion of Turkey. Yugoslavia has been breaking up since 1991, leading to several wars.

Some of the Players in the Recent Balkan Wars

Serbs   **Eastern Orthodox Christians.**
Ancient enemies of **Moslems** and
Croats. In Bosnia, outnumbered by
Moslems. Ancient allies of Russia.

Moslems   Ancient enemies of **Serbs** and Croats.
In Bosnia, outgunned by Serbs; ancient
allies of **Turks** (Moslems).

Croats   Catholics. Ancient enemies of Serbs
and Moslems. In World War II, sided
with Germans against Serbs and
Russians.

Russians Eastern Orthodox Christians. Ancient
enemies of Moslems, especially Turks.
Allies of Serbs.

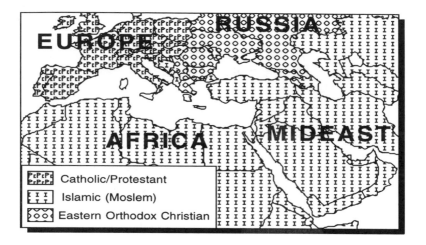

Catholic/Protestant

Islamic (Moslem)

Eastern Orthodox Christian

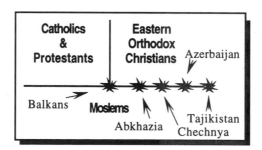

This schematic is derived from the map above. The homelands of the three groups form a rough inverted T. During the 1990s, no less than five wars broke out along the borders. The worst is in the Balkans where the three religions intersect. This intersection is why the Balkans have long been one of the bloodiest places on earth, possibly surpassed only by the Holy Land in the number of deaths per acre of ground.

But now our government leaders have turned deaf ears to the warnings of America's founders. They ignore the wisdom in George Washington's FAREWELL ADDRESS:

..."a passionate attachment of one nation for another produces a variety of evils. Sympathy for the favorite nation, facilitating the illusion of a imaginary common interest in cases where no real common interest exists, and infusion into one the enmities of the other, betrays the former into a participation in the quarrels and wars of the latter, without adequate inducement or justification. It leads also to concession to the favorite nation or privileges denied to others, which is apt doubly to injure the nation making the concessions, by unnecessarily parting with what ought to have been retained, *and by exciting jealousy, ill-will and a disposition to retaliate in the parties from whom equal privileges are withheld."* (emphasis mine.)

Washington called it retaliation, today's politicians call it terrorism.

From our prior sets of letters[5] you now understand the economic and legal models for making sense of the history we are about to explore. So, let's begin.

First, I will write about the root causes and terminology, then cover essential points of the history. At the end I will give my usual summary. I suggest you keep a world map or globe nearby so that you can more easily follow this wide-ranging story.

---

[5] Uncle Eric is referring to WHATEVER HAPPENED TO PENNY CANDY? and WHATEVER HAPPENED TO JUSTICE? by Richard J. Maybury, Bluestocking Press, Placerville, CA, 95667.

As usual, Chris, my main goal will be to give you the other side of the story, the **non-statist** side that you are not likely to hear anywhere else.   American culture today is almost entirely **statist.**

Uncle Eric

2

Three Root Causes

Dear Chris,

There is an old saying: "the first casualty of war is truth." I hope that in these letters we can do our part to rescue the truth.

I see three root causes of the U.S. involvement in the Mideast war. The first and most important is the refusal of all parties to see the situation from the other side's point of view.

This refusal is natural in any conflict, and on top of it is the fact that powerseekers on both sides wish to prevent understanding. Islamic leaders call us The Great Satan, and our leaders call them terrorists. Citizens and soldiers on both sides believe this propaganda and fail to look deeper. Filled with fear, and desperate for protection, they willingly give more power to the powerseekers, as they do in every war. The powerseekers get what they want, and the citizens and soldiers fill the cemeteries.

During this century until 1981, the number of Americans killed in the Mideast war was only a dozen or so. We might count Robert Kennedy as the first American casualty. In 1968 he was killed by Jordanian-born Sirhan Sirhan after announcing he wanted to send fifty F-4 jet fighters to Israel.

Now, after the bombing of Pan Am flight 103, and the Iraq-Kuwait war, the World Trade Center blasts and many other such incidents, American deaths total many hundreds, and the number injured is in the thousands.

America has suffered more losses in this war than in the Vietnam war through 1964, but not until 1998 did U.S. officials admit we are in another war. After the 1998 missile attacks on targets in Afghanistan and Sudan, Secretary of State Madeline Albright admitted, "This is, unfortunately, the war of the future."

But instead of "war," the common term remains "terrorism." This word sticks because the enemy is still fighting mostly with unconventional weapons and tactics such as hijackings, truck bombs, kidnappings, and attacks on embassies.

The enemy does not have battleships, intercontinental missiles or stealth bombers. If they did, these would surely be their weapons of choice. They use what they have.

Chris, terrorism is one of the most emotionally charged words in the English language. To call a person a **terrorist** is to call him a homicidal maniac. An individual is accused, tried and convicted with that single word. A "terrorist" is perceived as an irrational murderer who has *no reasonable cause* for his hatred.

The word terrorist supplies soldiers, sailors and airmen with a one-word explanation for why they are risking their lives in far-off lands. "Why am I here? To fight terrorism."

As long as officials continue to use this word, the American soldiers, sailors and airmen who fight and die in the Mideast will not be inclined to ask deeper questions about why they are risking their lives.

Why would officials do this? Because powerseekers on both sides wish to prevent understanding.

This points to the second root cause of the Mideast war, **political power**. I believe it corrupts both the morals and the judgment.

I wrote about political power in our prior set of letters about law and economic prosperity. (By the way, this might be a good time to review letters 26 and 27 from WHATEVER HAPPENED TO JUSTICE?[6])

Political power is the legal privilege of using force on persons who have not harmed anyone.

This privilege is what sets government apart from all other institutions. And, it is what political powerseekers are seeking, whether they understand, or openly admit this, or not.

I believe political power is the most deadly, addicting narcotic ever discovered. Let me explain.

A powerseeker spends his life trying to acquire power. Once he has it, he naturally wants to use it on someone.

In America, however, the **Bill of Rights** is a barrier that often prevents a powerseeker from using his privilege on his fellow Americans.

But, the Bill of Rights stops at the border. It does not protect foreigners.

So, American powerseekers often turn their attention toward foreigners.

For instance, expanding their "sphere of influence" during the **Cold War**, U.S. powerseekers helped anyone who claimed to be anti-Soviet and pro-American. The Shah of Iran, Noriega in Panama, Marcos in the Philippines, Batista in Cuba, Diem in Vietnam, the Samozas in Nicaragua — the list of "pro-American" cutthroats goes on for pages.

---

[6] Uncle Eric is referring to WHATEVER HAPPENED TO JUSTICE? by Richard J. Maybury, Bluestocking Press, Placerville, CA, 95667.

Chris, as long as these tyrants claimed to be anti-Soviet and pro-American they received money, weapons and military training from U.S. officials. *This did not make us popular with their victims.*

I once asked an audience of about 150 people this question:

> "How many of you have had a friend or member of your family tortured, kidnapped or killed by the U.S. government or by a regime backed by the U.S. government? Raise your hands."[7]

Four hands went up. I pointed out that in some countries, half or more of the audience would have raised their hands. The leading candidate would be Iran. The U.S. backed the Shah of Iran and his murderous secret police for 25 years, then backed Iraq's Saddam Hussein when Hussein attacked Iran.

Why? Because these enemies of the Iranian people *claimed* to be pro-American. (For more on Iran and Iraq, see the Appendix.)

Today the Cold War appears to have ended — at least it does at the moment I am writing this — but the practice of aiding foreign **dictators** has not. The U.S. has troops in 144 countries, [8] which is about two-thirds of all the countries on earth. In most cases, the troops are there to help train the troops of those governments.

---

[7] Asked of the Eris Society meeting in Aspen, Colorado on August 6, 1998.

[8] Air Force Times, August 3, 1998, p.31

The world is a nasty place. Only about two dozen governments are limited enough that an American would feel safe living under them without the escape hatch of an American passport.[9] Watch the excellent Richard Gere movie RED CORNER[10] and you will know what most other countries are like.

Washington backs the two dozen *and* at least 120 others, and no one is sure why, except that these 120 governments *claim* to be pro-American.

During the 1990s, U.S. officials even began backing the Kremlin, supplying it with money and military training.

The Kremlin has lots of enemies.

Now the Kremlin's enemies are our enemies.

Why do American powerseekers do this? Those of us who have no interest in political power have a hard time understanding persons who have the addiction. The best explanation I can offer concerns the game of chess.

Most of the pleasure in chess comes from the playing, not the winning. Chess players will play even when they know they are sure to lose. They enjoy the maneuvering, strategy, risks and sacrifices.

This is what political power is like except that the pieces being maneuvered and sacrificed are not plastic or wood, they are humans.

Political power is the game of playing God. It changes a person and makes him different from the rest of us. He begins to believe he has some kind of right to interfere in the lives of others. He may even believe he has the right to choose who lives and who dies.

---

[9] With an American passport, one can quickly jump on a plane and escape back to America. The native citizens cannot do this.

[10] R rated.

For a thousand years, European rulers have played this game in the Mideast. Their pawns have been the Moslems, Christians and Jews who live there.

Now the Moslem pawns have begun to rebel and European rulers are backing out of the game. U.S. rulers have stepped in to take their place. And, I believe, as in chess, the objective is the joy of playing; winning is incidental. Even though losing appears highly likely, our powerseekers continue to play.

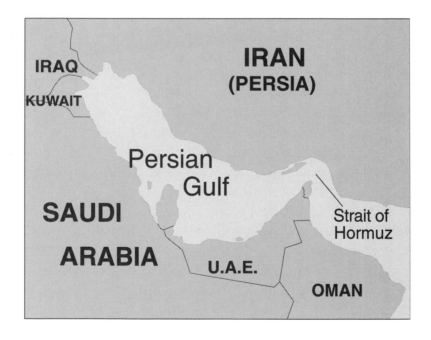

65% of the total world oil supply is in the Persian Gulf. Saudi Arabia has the largest oil fields and has exerted the most influence on the supply and price.

The State Department and other agencies contain career historians hired for their expert knowledge of the Islamic world. Occasionally one of these experts will express frustration about politicians ignoring their warnings. For more than thirty years the powerseekers have been plunging us ever deeper into a conflict that makes little sense, and these experts know it.

In her widely acclaimed 1986 book SACRED RAGE[11], award winning Mideast reporter Robin Wright did an excellent job of summarizing these warnings. No one in government seems to have heard.

To heed the warnings is to abandon the game. What chess player wants to do that?

> *"The world's oil stability rests in the hands of one tired and ailing man — Saudi Arabia's King Fahd. For over 30 years he has single-handedly manipulated Saudi production to meet American demand and price objectives. His successor, Prince Abdullah, has vowed to put Islamic interests first."*
>
> ENERGY INVESTOR, August 1998

History repeats. In a survey of 108 Army generals at the end of the Vietnam war, 70% said the government's objectives in Vietnam were unclear, and 52% said the stated objectives could not be achieved.[12]

Think about it, 58,000 Americans were killed and 153,000 wounded for reasons not even generals could understand.

We are doing it again in the Mideast, playing the game.

---

[11] SACRED RAGE by Robin Wright, Simon & Schuster.
[12] WALL STREET JOURNAL, January 14, 1985.

Thousands of Soviet troops died in Afghanistan, and hundreds of Americans have died in Lebanon, as well as in the Persian Gulf and "terrorist" incidents, but I am afraid this new chess game is only just beginning.

Chris, the third root cause of U.S. entanglement in the Mideast is very simple, and you already know about it — violation of the two fundamental laws, especially the second law: "Do not encroach on other persons or their property." Every government involved in the Mideast violates this law and has for centuries.

I know I am writing

> *"Resistance to the U.S. presence in Saudi Arabia by some of the kingdom's most influential figures has been largely ignored in the West. ... What the so-called terrorist experts routinely fail to discuss are the reasons for Muslim frustration: Palestinian dispossession, American domination of the Arab world, Washington's blind support for Israel, the U.S. stranglehold on the Persian Gulf oil market, and so on. ... Saudi Arabia is metamorphosing into an anti-American nation in front of our eyes."*
> *— Robert Fisk, London* INDEPENDENT, *August 9, 1998*

some harsh words here, but I offer no apology. As I said in my first letter, my goal is to give you the other side of the story, the non-statist side that is based on the two fundamental laws I wrote about in my previous letters. America is in a war, this subject is much too serious for polite, cocktail party chatter.

Uncle Eric

> *"The big men on both sides kill for power. They kill to rule."*
>
> *— Sister of fallen Afghan soldier*

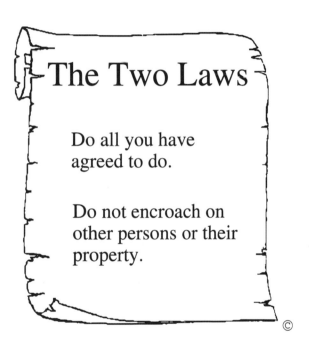

The two laws that make civilization possible.

3

Muddying the Waters

Dear Chris,

Powerseekers on both sides do all they can to muddy the waters. They are helped by the fact that most of the languages of the Islamic world are not easily translated into English. Pronunciations, written characters and definitions are outside our experience.

Here are some examples of the confusing language. Israelis say Israel is a "Jewish state." What, exactly, is a Jewish state? No one seems to know, or at least no two Jews would offer the same definition, but Israeli Jews are proud of their "Jewish state."

U.S. officials insist on referring to the problems in Israel as the "Arab-Israeli conflict." This leads us to assume Arab is the opposite of Jew.

The fact is that **Arab** refers to race and **Jew** refers to religion. Check your dictionary, Arabs are **Semites**; *some Jews are Arabs.*

Also, in America, the term **anti-Semite** is assumed to mean anti-Jewish. But, since Arabs, too, are Semites, anti-Semite can mean anti-Arab.

Semite means a person descended from Noah's son Shem. This includes Hebrews, Arabs, Assyrians, Phoenicians and others.

The frequent use of the word Arab is itself misleading. Race has almost nothing to do with Mideast politics. The primary factor in the Mideast is religion. The Mideast war is a religious war much like those of Europe during the Middle Ages.

The word **Mideast** can be misleading, too. Its strict definition means the region from Egypt to Afghanistan but (follow this on your globe or world map) the Islamic world is enormous, encompassing dozens of countries from Morocco to the Philippines, and from the equator to deep in the former Soviet Union.

We cannot even agree on the correct name for the Islamic peoples who inhabit these areas. Moslem, Muslim, Moor, Morisco, Mohammedan, Mussulman, Moro and Saracen have all been used at one time or another.

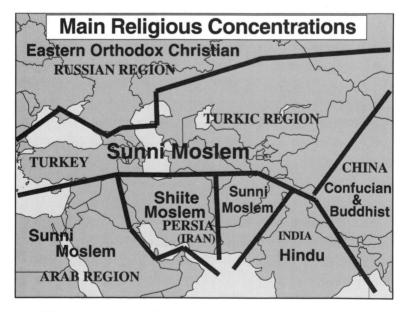

Although every nation contains individual members of many religions, these are the main religious concentrations in Asia.

The religion is **Islam** but Islam is also a political system. Mohammed taught that no government's law is valid unless it agrees with the law of Allah (God).

Chris, I am not comfortable with any of the available terminology related to this war, but to communicate I must use terminology of some kind, so here is what I will do. I will speak of Islam as the opponent in this war, and **Moslems** as the people who practice the Islamic religion.

We need a term for the side you and I have been born on. Moslems seem to focus their hatred primarily against the U.S., Russia, Britain, France and Israel, and secondarily against other Europeans, and they refer to this side as "**The West**." The term is not accurate. Russia may be in Europe but it stretches farther east than China; Morocco, an Islamic nation, is farther west than England.

However, I don't know of a better term than The West, so in this set of letters, Chris, our side will be called The West, even though it includes Russia, and I will call their side "**the Islamic world**." This war is The West vs. the Islamic world.

> *"Most of the killing taking place around the world in recent years has been caused by religious conflict. ... Religious fundamentalism, long suppressed by the Cold War, [is] now bursting forth in all righteous and murderous rage."*
>
> Arthur Schlesinger, Jr.
> WALL STREET JOURNAL, 11/22/95

Let me hasten to add that not all Moslems hate us. Many Moslems in the Mideast are friendly toward us and distressed about the war. Also, more than three million[13] Moslems live in the U.S.

---

[13] This number is difficult to pin down, reports vary. The Statistical Abstract of the United States reports 5.5 million Moslems in North America.

But, the battle lines have been drawn, Islam against the West, and I have seen no evidence that powerseekers on either side are willing to back off. They want us all to choose sides, neutrality is not permitted.

Chris, I am afraid the hardest choices will be faced by American Moslems. These people will be forced to choose between their country and their religion. In fact, I fear we all will eventually. No major religion today sanctions religious war, but this is exactly what our rulers have plunged us into.

Make your choice, your God or your government, you can't follow both when they are headed in opposite directions.

Uncle Eric

Watch for this Eagle

The two-headed eagle was the sign of the Byzantine Empire. Looking both east and west, it symbolized control of the Bosporus Strait. After the Byzantine Empire, which was Christian, was overrun by the Moslem Turks, Russians assumed leadership of the Christian world against the Moslem world and adopted the two-headed eagle as their symbol. Now Russian nationalists are reviving this symbol.

THE WALL STREET JOURNAL has run a story about Turkey using environmental concerns as an excuse to restrict Russia's access to the Bosporus. Could anything be more likely to start a world war?

History certainly does repeat. Watch for the two-headed eagle,[14] the more you see of it, the closer we are to a major shootout between the Christian and Moslem worlds.

And, warn everyone you care about. If they don't hear about it from you they probably won't hear about it until it's too late.

---

[14] The two-headed eagle is used in other contexts, too. For instance, it appears on the flag of Albania, and Albania is a Moslem nation. But when the two-headed eagle appears in conjunction with Russia or with issues relating to the Black Sea and Bosporus Strait, it is ominous.

4

How Many?

Dear Chris,

After my last few letters I am sure you are wondering where my loyalties lie. Whose side is Uncle Eric on, really?

I am loyal to the two fundamental laws taught by all religions: do all you have agreed to do, and do not encroach on other persons or their property.

This means I am on the side of anyone who obeys these laws, regardless of his or her religion, race, language or nationality.

I do not know any government that obeys these laws, so I am not on the side of any government.

I am solidly on the side of the millions of individuals in every country who obey these two laws.

And, speaking of religion, this is something I think a lot about, it is central to the Thousand Year War. I have seen many individuals derive great benefit from religion, and I have seen others hurt by it. In most cases the difference, I think, is the two laws. When an individual's religion is used to bolster these laws, the results can be wonderful. When religion is used to undermine these laws, the result is often disastrous, as today's religious wars in east Europe, Asia and Africa demonstrate so horribly. Total deaths from these wars during the 1990s numbered in the millions.

Again, if you obey the two laws, I am on your side, whatever your race, language, religion or country.

Now, on to your question. In your most recent letter, Chris, you asked, "How many Moslems are there?" No one knows. I have seen estimates as low as 600 million and as high as 1.1 billion.

We do know most live in the enormous region stretching from Morocco to the Philippines, and from the equator to northern Kazakhstan.

For comparison, the total population of the U.S. is about 270 million, the population of Russia is 148 million, and Israel 5.5 million.

Add the population of the non-Russian part of Europe, which is about 360 million, and we can see the war is between two roughly equal populations which comprise roughly a third of mankind living on four continents (North America, Europe, Africa, Asia).

In other words, this is a world war.

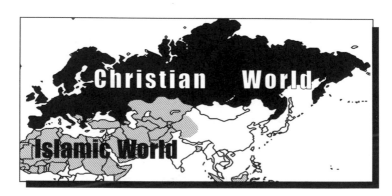

Further complicating the war is the fact that 50 million Moslems live inside the former Soviet Union, in many cases right alongside the Russians. They have no love for the Russians, who are Eastern Orthodox Christian and who conquered them and forced them into the Soviet Union, and who still dominate most of the governments of the former Soviet states.

Inspired by the two successful Moslem uprisings against the Russians, in Afghanistan and Chechnya, these 50 million Moslems would like nothing better than to blow the Kremlin off the face of the earth. They and their ancestors have felt this way for centuries.

This is a very big and unimaginably messy situation, and it offers no clear way to divide good guys from bad guys.

Now, let's explore the history and motivations of the Islamic struggle against the West.

Uncle Eric

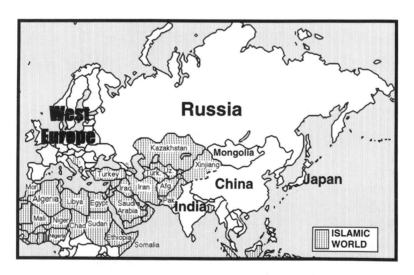

The Moslem religion is Islam. Moslems have been known by many names: Muslim, Mohammedan, Moor, Morisco, Saracen and others. For more than a thousand years the Islamic world and Christian Europeans have fought. Since the Middle Ages there has rarely been a five-year period in which European troops have not been under arms on Moslem soil.

Moslem Populations
Estimated Millions
1997

Albania	2.3	Libya	5.4
Algeria	30	Malaysia	8
Azerbaijan	7.3	Mali	9
Bangladesh	111	Mauritania	2.4
Benin	.9	Morocco	30
Bosnia & Herzegovina	1.2	Niger	7.5
Chad	3.5	Nigeria	54
China	31	Pakistan	128
Dijibouti	.4	Philippines	3.8
Egypt	61	Russia	unknown
Ethiopia	28	Saudi Arabia	20
Gambia	1.1	Senegal	8.6
Ghana	5.4	Sierra Leone	3
Guinea - (Bissau)	.36	Sudan	23
India	135	Syria	12
Indonesia	183	Tajikistan	5
Iran	67	Togo	.5
Iraq	22	Tunisia	9
Israel	.8	Turkey	63
Jordan	4	Turkmenistan	3.7
Kazakhstan	8	Uzbekistan	21
Liberia	.5	U.S.	6.5
		Western Sahara	.2

Much of this data comes from the CIA website. At the time of this writing the URL is www.odci.gov/cia/publications/factbook/

5

How Would You React?

Dear Chris,

You mentioned several times that you enjoyed my set of letters about the CLIPPER SHIP STRATEGY[15]. Using a physical object like a ship to illustrate a lesson makes it easy to remember and use the lesson.

Here's another case where I can use a ship to make a point.

Docked at Lahina on the island of Maui in Hawaii is a small sailing ship called the Carthaginian. This two-masted brig appears to be from the 1700s but it was built in Germany after World War I when the rest of Europe was in the era of giant steamships like the Queen Mary. In the attempt to keep the Germans subservient, British and French rulers had restricted their capacity to rebuild their economy. Germans were allowed to manufacture ships no longer than 100 feet with no more than 35 horsepower — that of a motorcycle engine. The Queen Mary was 1,020 feet and over 100,000 horsepower. Germans had no choice but to revert to wind power.

---

[15] Uncle Eric is referring to THE CLIPPER SHIP STRATEGY by Richard J. Maybury, Bluestocking Press, PO Box 1014, Placerville, CA 95667.

The reprisals also involved trade restrictions and reparations including the confiscation of rail equipment, coal fields and machinery as well as huge cash payments.

The German economy was ravaged by the British and French, and thousands of Germans were left with no way to earn a living or support their families. As one of my uncles, a veteran of World War II said, "British and French rulers got the Germans down on the ground with their boots on their throats and wouldn't let them up."

After fifteen years of this brutal treatment, the desperate Germans, experiencing 40% unemployment, became irrational. They embraced Hitler and his gangsters as saviors. We all know the result, and British and French rulers were at least as responsible as the Germans.

> *If there is one thing government loves above all else, it is crisis. Crisis provides the opportunity to write laws, create programs, increase taxes, spend money, expand the bureaucracy, impose regulations, extend control — in short, to justify more government."*
> *Jim Lord*
> *Y2K Survival Letter*
> *October 1998*

Knowing what caused the Germans to go insane, try to imagine, Chris, how people would react if they had been treated this way, not for fifteen years, but for a thousand. How would you react?

This is what's been happening in the Mideast, and it's why we are experiencing the so-called terrorism. European rulers have been brutalizing Moslems for a thousand years and now the Moslems are again beginning to strike back. This is not to condone the murder of innocent people, it is only to say the cycle of murder and reprisal was started by the rulers of Europe.

Uncle Eric

6

Three Religions

Dear Chris,

Palestine is another name for the so-called Holy Land on the eastern shore of the Mediterranean. This area is sacred to all three major Biblical religions — **Christianity, Judaism** and **Islam**. Judaism is the oldest of the three and Islam is the newest.

All three religions regard Abraham as their patriarch.

Jews and Christians trace their descent from Abraham's son **Isaac**. Moslems trace their descent from Abraham's son **Ishmael**.

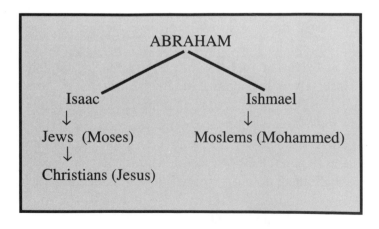

All three revere the Bible and believe in its God, and regard Jerusalem as a hallowed city.

The leading prophet of the Jews was **Moses**, who died around 1200 B.C.

The leader of the Christians was **Jesus**, who died around 29 A.D.

The leader of the Moslems was **Mohammed** who died in 632 A.D.

Members of all three groups have lived in the Holy Land continuously since Biblical times. Political dominance has shifted among them. Presently the Jews hold sway, they have established the Jewish state called Israel.

Chris, as I mentioned in an earlier letter, don't ask what a Jewish state is, the term is vague and no two Jews agree. All we know is that the Jews are proud of it and the Moslems hate it. (The present Christian population is small and generally doesn't say much.)

How would you feel if you were, say, Presbyterian, and you were told that you would have to live under a Baptist state? My guess is you'd first say, what's a Baptist state?, then you'd say, I don't care what it is, I refuse to live under it.

Of course, the Jews weren't too happy when the Moslems were running the place, and neither was happy when the Christians were. In fact, the state of Israel was established in 1948 after a rebellion against the British who were Christian.

In short, the Holy Land is a dramatic example of the fact that in the Mideast, religion is politics.

This is, incidentally, also a good example why America's founders *began* the Bill of Rights with the statement, "Congress shall make no law respecting an establishment of Religion, or prohibiting the free exercise thereof." The founders said *no* law. No law for, no law against, no law period. The founders knew that once a government makes a law in favor of one religion or against another, the country is headed down the road to endless bloodshed.

In Jerusalem's Church of the Holy Sepulcher, a ladder stands beneath some windows. When three Christian sects agreed to joint administration of the church, they said from that point on there would be no changes to the church. At the moment the agreement was signed, a workman happened to be washing the windows. His ladder has stayed in that exact spot ever since, for more than 140 years.

Uncle Eric

7

They Think Differently

Dear Chris,

Why do we in the West fail to understand the Mideast? One reason was pointed out by Egyptian president Anwar Sadat just before he was assassinated in 1981. Sadat said Americans would never understand the Mideast because the Mideast is so old, whereas America is so young.

Jericho is the world's most ancient city. Many Moslems will cite archaeologists who say Jericho goes back 10,000 years.

American civilization is only about 450 years old, so, measured against this 10,000-year Moslem time clock, American civilization is still in its infancy, only 4.5% the age of the Mideast. The U.S. itself is even younger, only 2% the age of the Mideast.

This is more important than it sounds. Having the world's newest civilization, Americans have an unusually brief time perspective. To us, something that happened fifty years ago falls under the category of "old." It is a bygone, we've forgotten about it and forgiven everyone involved. In 1945 we were at war with the Japanese and Germans, now we are friends.

Chris, this isn't to say past events do not affect us. They do, we carry a lot of baggage. But American culture is young, very forward looking and founded on the two laws, so we try to jettison the baggage whenever we can, we find it embarrassing.

In the Mideast, fifty years ago is just yesterday. To them, the founding of the state of Israel in 1948 falls under the category of current events.

It's not much of an exaggeration to say that in the Mideast there are no bygones. Any injury suffered in the past two thousand years is still fresh. Ask a Lebanese guerrilla why he fights and he is likely to say, "In 1842 their great-great grandfather killed my great-great grandfather."

Under these circumstances it's a piece of cake for a powerseeker to dig up reasons why people should hate each other and go to war. Every individual on this planet has an ancestor who hurt someone at one time or another.

This difference in time perspectives is also why Americans see each Mideast conflict as a separate war while Moslems see them as chapters in the same war. We think in terms of "we'll do this to them at 3:30 pm, that at 4:45 pm and that at 6:15 pm." They think in terms of "we'll do this to them in 1999, that in 2000, and that in 2001."

Incidentally, one tactical military result of this difference in time perspectives is that people in the Mideast have more patience than we do. For them, waiting years to retaliate is entirely normal. In 1986, the U.S. bombed Tripoli; two years later, Pan Am flight 103 was blown up.

Uncle Eric

8

The Lost Civilization

Dear Chris,

The conflict in the Holy Land is only a small part of the larger war between the West and Islam, but this small conflict was the beginning of the larger one; we need to examine it closely.

The story begins in the 5th and 6th centuries. The Roman empire was disintegrating and the Romans were at war with the **Persians. Persia** is **Iran.**

As you may recall from my previous set of letters[16], the constant turmoil and massive arbitrary power of the Roman government had reduced the Roman legal system to a confused mush. With no rational legal framework on which to base agreements, business people could not plan ahead and the Mediterranean economy was in chaos. Europe's "Dark Ages" were beginning.

A well traveled, highly intelligent businessman, known to his associates as The Trustworthy One, decided something had to be done. To straighten out the law, he reasoned

---

[16] Uncle Eric is referring to ANCIENT ROME: HOW IT AFFECTS YOU TODAY, by Richard J. Maybury, Bluestocking Press, Placerville, CA 95667.

it would be necessary to revive the old Biblical idea of a Higher Law than human law.

To accomplish this legal reform the businessman invented a new religion which quickly became popular among the Arab peoples around the Mediterranean. The businessman was Mohammed and this new religion was "Islam," which means "submission" to God's law.

Under this new legal code the economy of the Mediterranean world began to recover, and by the year 750 it had achieved what historians call the Arab-Moslem Golden Age.

However, Mohammed's followers were as human as the rest of us and their political power affected them exactly as it does anyone else. Often they made conversions to Islam by the sword rather than by peaceful persuasion. Moslem cavalry emerged from Arabia to spread Islam across a vast expanse, from Spain to Persia.

This early militaristic period has given Islam an undeserved reputation for being inherently warlike. The basic philosophy is no more warlike than that of Christianity or any other religion. And, most Moslems today are peaceful and gentle despite the fact that in many cases European rulers have pushed them to the breaking point.

After all, where did the two worst wars[17] in history begin? They began in Europe, between Christians. But no one claims Christianity was the cause. It's the same with Islam.

The fiery early period of Islamic conquest gave way to a more mature and gracious civilization, and this new civilization was the most advanced ever known until ours today.

In fact, Chris, it was the forerunner of ours today. Americans are taught that we inherited our way of life from Europe, and this is true to a large extent. But Islam gave us

---

[17] The two world wars.

at least as much as Europe did, although **Europhiles**[18] are in no hurry to broadcast this fact.

Fortunately, in his fine book MAINSPRING OF HUMAN PROGRESS, Henry Grady Weaver gave us the story of Islam's contribution to our civilization, which I will draw from shortly.

I am forever amazed at the way some Americans who would never dream of uttering a racist remark about Blacks, Mexicans or Chinese will refer openly to Arab Moslems as ragheads, camel jockeys or some other slur, and even laugh about it. For some, **Eurocentric**[19] propaganda has been so successful that "Arab terrorist" has become a single word. Few Americans understand what we owe to the Arab Moslems. Many seem to see inhabitants of the Islamic world as primitive, unwashed, fanatical and violent.

On the contrary, the **Koran** encourages intellectual inquiry, and Islam contains the world's oldest college, al-Azhar in Cairo.

> *"Prejudices against Muslims — and the spread of ludicrously inaccurate stereotypes — have been developing at a frightening rate during the past decade. Anti-Muslim racism seems in many ways to be replacing anti-Semitism. ... Perhaps the most worrying thing about this trend is the extent to which it has gone unrecognized and uncriticized while intellectual versions of anti-Islamic revulsion have found acceptance in defense and political circles. NATO's former secretary general, Willy Claes, told the German daily SUDDEUTSCHE ZEITUNG: 'Islamic fundamentalism is just as much a threat to the West as communism was.'"*
>
> THE OBSERVER, *London 4/21/96*

---

[18] One who admires Europe.

[19] Centered or focused on Europe. The European viewpoint.

During the centuries when Europe was mired in the poverty and ignorance of the Dark Ages, the Islamic world was a beacon of light moving rapidly ahead through advancements in science and technology. These advancements eventually spread to Europe, causing the Renaissance, then to America.

The numbers we use today are not Roman numerals, they are Arabic.

The navigation instruments and charts Columbus used to discover the new world were derived from those of the Moslems.

The Spanish architecture we see in America's southwest was learned from the Moslems.

You might have seen this depicted in the Kevin Costner movie ROBIN HOOD: PRINCE OF THIEVES. Robin's sidekick was a Moslem who was more educated and knowledgeable about science and technology than the Europeans among whom he traveled. In those days, the universities of Moslem-controlled Spain were the prime destination of Europe's scholars.

You see, Chris, the science and technology of the ancient Roman world had been lost by the Europeans, but the Moslems rescued it.

In that era, the Europeans referred to the Moslems as **Saracens**, meaning barbarians. Europeans typically bathed once a year, the Saracens every day.

While Europe was in continual famine due to primitive farming practices, Saracen farmers were fertilizing, contour-plowing, irrigating and rotating crops.

A medieval European typically lived his entire life in a single place never traveling or knowing anything about the world beyond his village. Even kings and queens were illiterate.

Under the legal reforms instituted by Mohammed, the Saracens (Arab Moslems) created a highly advanced civilization. Theirs was the most prosperous on earth, far ahead of the Europeans who were living in the poverty and ignorance of the Dark Ages. Or at least this civilization was the most prosperous until...

The Moslems were educated and they engaged in vigorous commerce from France to China. Their mail was delivered by a pony express system faster than our postal system today. For urgent communications they used air express — carrier pigeons.

The Moslems preserved and gave us Aristotle's logic. Try to imagine today's world without logic.

They built medical schools and gave us surgery, anesthesia and pharmacology. From them we received cotton clothing, asphalt paving, beds, strawberries and ice-cream.

Author Rose Wilder Lane[20] wrote, "Our cars run, our streets are paved, our houses are furnished and our bodies clothed with things that the Saracens created."

The Europeans may be our ancestors by blood but the Moslems are our ancestors by intellect. To learn more about this great civilization, read Rose Wilder Lane's THE DISCOVERY OF FREEDOM, as well as MAINSPRING OF HUMAN PROGRESS by Henry Grady Weaver.

Incidentally, many of these advancements in science and technology were made by Moslems and Jews working together. Jewish contributions to our modern civilization have been massive, yet they remain as unappreciated as those of the Moslems.

Again, Chris, I know I am being harsh, especially when talking about the rulers of Europe, but this war is serious business — harsh business — and these letters may be your only chance to hear the non-statist side of the story.

Uncle Eric

---

[20] From THE DISCOVERY OF FREEDOM by Rose Wilder Lane, published by Fox and Wilkes, San Francisco, CA. Rose Wilder Lane was the daughter of Laura Ingalls Wilder. Rose spent the last twenty years of her life studying the history of individual liberty which culminated in her book THE DISCOVERY OF FREEDOM.

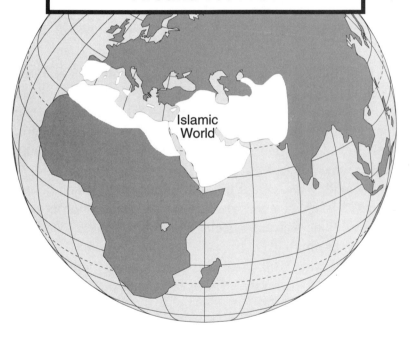

Islamic World During Arab-Moslem Golden Age

Around 750 A.D.

Islamic World

9

The European Attack

Dear Chris,

I call the war we are in today the **Thousand Year War**. It began during the time of Pope Sylvester II who lived from 940 to 1003 A.D. This was a period when Moslems had control of the Holy Land and Pope Sylvester didn't like it. He believed Christians should run the place and began laying plans to make it so.

Around 970 A.D., Emperors Nicephorus Phocas and John Zimisces attacked Moslems in the area which is now Turkey. Pope Sylvester decided they had a great idea, and began to promote it.

By the year 1095 the idea had become popular, and preparations for a massive European attack on the Moslems had been completed.

The **Crusades** began. Wave after wave of Europeans rolled through the Moslem civilization in a hurricane of death and destruction that lasted two centuries.

These campaigns were some of the most savage in history and they did almost as much damage in Europe as they did to the Moslems. In launching the Crusades, Pope Urban had told the Crusaders that one reward for their valor would be that all their sins would be forgiven when they entered battle in the Holy Land. The Crusaders decided this meant they could do anything they wanted on the way to the Holy Land and all would be forgiven.

...the European Crusaders arrived from the West.

When European rulers set out to establish their empires, the Moslems were the first people they went after because the Moslems were the closest to them.

The amount of rape, pillage and murder they committed in Europe on their journey toward Palestine was so awful entire European towns were wiped out.

By the time the Europeans got to the Holy Land they had become an army of bloodthirsty butchers. Whole cities were leveled and thousands of men, women and children were tortured and murdered. Large land areas were depopulated.

In the two-year siege of Acre, 100,000 Moslems were killed. At Jerusalem the Archbishop of Tyre declared "the city presented a spectacle of such slaughter of enemies and shedding of blood that it struck the conquerors themselves with horror and disgust."[21]

When 10,000 terrified, helpless Moslems took refuge in the Mosque of Soliman, all were slaughtered.

Not satisfied with butchering children, babies and the aged, the Europeans even killed pets, livestock and zoo animals.

When the Europeans arrived in Egypt, the Moslem city of Damietta was a thriving commercial center inhabited by 70,000 prosperous individuals. When they left, Damietta was a ruins haunted by 3,000 sick and starving wretches. The site was eventually abandoned.

[21] The Medieval and Rennaissance World, edited by Esmond Wright, Chartwell Books, Secaucus, New Jersey, 1979, p.92

All across the Mideast, desert encroached on once fertile farm land as the most advanced civilization ever seen on earth up to that time was demolished.

But the holocaust of death and destruction did not end there. Europe's Crusades have never ended. They evolved into the Inquisition which robbed, tortured and murdered Moslems and Jews until Napoleon halted it in 1808.

But the Crusades did not satisfy European Rulers. Under their Inquisition, the robbery, torture and murder of Moslems and Jews continued until the 1800s.

The Inquisition evolved into the Barbary Wars, and the Barbary Wars evolved into the European colonial conquests during the nineteenth and twentieth centuries.

Chris, what I'm about to tell you is very important. If you remember nothing else from these letters, remember the following, it is the root cause of nearly all the bloodshed and economic turmoil connected with the Mideast today. *Not since the Middle Ages have Moslem armies threatened an invasion of Europe, but since that time there has hardly been any five-year period in which European troops have not been under arms on Moslem soil.*[22]

But think about it. We often see people pray and practice faith based on events that happened hundreds or thousands of years ago. Religious faith is seen as a good thing, so we are not surprised at this attachment to ancient events. Hatred can be every bit as strong as religious faith, and it can go back just as far. In the Old World, grudges are commonly passed from generation to generation just as carefully as sacred rituals are.

Now, before we go further, please check any encyclopedia for a map of the European colonial empires before World War II. In the 1997 computerized Grolier Encyclopedia, for instance, look under "colonialism," and check the map of Africa.

Moslems weren't alone, European rulers were using most of mankind as chess pawns.

---

[22] Godfrey Jansen quoted in SACRED RAGE by Robin Wright, published by Simon & Schuster, 1986, p.252

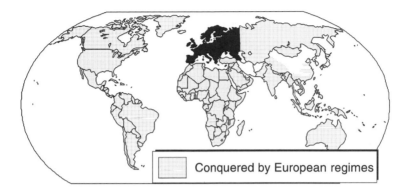

Conquered by European regimes

Europe is small, only 6.6% of the earth's land surface, but Europeans inherited the Roman lust for conquest and one world government. In the Crusades they set out to satisfy this lust, attacking their nearest neighbors, the Moslems. Their addiction to power grew until by the 1960s they had attacked and conquered nearly everyone on earth. The only countries able to beat them off were Persia (Iran), China, Afghanistan, Thailand and Japan, and the first four took a terrible pounding. In some cases the Europeans used their own troops, and in others they used surrogates. In the conquered countries, surrogate regimes were established to serve European ends. Today most of the world's political landscape is a botched up mess left over from the European conquests. The Islamic world is the worst, it was closest to the Europeans and received the worst pounding, and for the longest period of time, a thousand years. Yet, Americans have been taught to be Europhiles.

Europe's Thousand Year War against the Moslems is one of the worst atrocities in history, it is in the same league as the Nazi persecution of the Jews, and as the Soviet Socialist extermination of millions of non-socialists. Moslems cannot forget it. To them the Crusades remain as real as if they had happened just yesterday, and these invasions have done much to shape the thinking of the people who live in and around the Persian Gulf oil fields.

Chris, during the Crusades the western invaders were called **Franj**, meaning French, and today this word is still used in colloquial Arabic to mean Westerner.

Castles built by Europeans in the Holy Land still stand as daily reminders of the holocaust that demolished the magnificent Islamic civilization. Moslems drive by them on their way to work.

This castle, the Krak des Chevaliers, was built by the European Crusaders and stands today as a reminder of what they did to the Moslems.

We Americans tend to assume each outbreak of violence is a different war. The rebellion against the French in Algeria in 1850 is seen by us as a different war than the rebellion against the British in the Sudan in 1885. The Soviet invasion of Afghanistan in 1979 is seen as a different conflict than the one that killed U.S. Marines in Lebanon in 1983. The Lebanon conflict is viewed as separate from the Iran-Iraq war in which the USS Stark was nearly sunk.

It's all the same war — the war it has always been — the Crusades, they never ended.

As the Deputy Prime Minister of Turkey once said, "**NATO**, the Common Market and the West in general are inspired by the spirit of the Crusades."[23] Libya's Qadaffi: "The West is mad! It is still with the spirit of the Crusades."[24]

You and I may not see it that way. They do.

European rulers have had their boots on the throats of Moslems for a thousand years. Can it be any wonder some Moslems are now reacting the way the Germans did in the 1930s?

Of course, some of the Moslem "terrorists" probably are genuine terrorists, this cannot be denied, or excused. They are barbarians who are in the fight just for the fun of inflicting pain. But don't judge all the Moslems by these few. Every army contains some of these types, wars naturally attract killers.

Most Moslems are no different than us or the Israelis. They are kind, gentle people who fight only when they have been driven to desperate measures.

The question is, who drove them there?

---

[23] THE DAGGER OF ISLAM, by John Laffin, Bantam, 1981, p.136
[24] U.S. NEWS & WORLD REPORT, November 10, 1986, p.32

The Arab oil dictators are backed and kept in power by the descendants of the Crusaders — by the governments of Britain, France and the U.S. Tens of millions of Moslems are livid over this and are not likely to tolerate it much longer. The effect on oil prices and investment markets will be profound.

Chris, you might go to a bookstore or library and get EXTRAORDINARY POPULAR DELUSIONS AND THE MADNESS OF CROWDS by Charles Mackay, and THE CRUSADES THROUGH ARAB EYES by Amin Maalouf. As you read Mackay's ninth chapter, and Maalouf's page 39, remember that Europe's bloodthirsty psychopaths nine centuries ago set the stage for today's relations between the Islamic world and the Christian West.

Then get the History Channel's videotape series titled CRUSADES (Item #AH13400). Call 800-708-1776. And, after you've watched that, ask a librarian for WORTH magazine's 11/95 article by Jim Rogers, "Tent of Saud."

People behave the way they do because they think the way they do, and they think the way they do because of their history. The more you know about the Crusades, the more you will understand what's probably coming in the economy, the oil fields and the investment markets.

Uncle Eric

10

The Barbary Wars

Dear Chris,

The story continues. The Marine Corps hymn contains the phrase "from the Halls of Montezuma to the shores of Tripoli." Why the shores of **Tripoli**?

The phrase refers to Libya's coast near the Gulf of Sidra. The **Gulf of Sidra** is where U.S. Navy jets shot down two Libyan jets in 1981, and where more clashes have occurred since. These were not the first battles between Washington and Moslems.

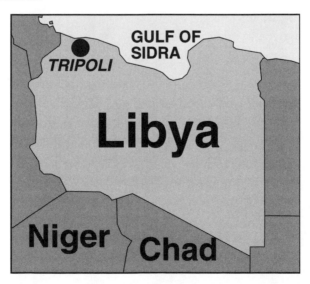

U.S. officials contend the Gulf of Sidra is international waters, but this area has been claimed by Moslems since the Middle Ages, long before there was any such thing as international law.

In those days many Moslems living in the **Barbary States** of North Africa were refugees from the European Inquisition, or descendants of persons killed by the Crusaders. They were levying a tax on European vessels sailing along the African coast.

European merchants somehow convinced their governments to pay this tax for them, so the Moslems knew they could make the tax quite heavy.

Resentful of the Crusades and Inquisition, the Moslems raised the tax frequently. Finally in 1801 the tiny American government could no longer afford to pay.

U.S. merchantmen continued sailing through the area anyhow, and the Pasha of Tripoli captured and imprisoned the tax evaders.

Chris, European rulers saw a golden opportunity. They called the Moslems pirates and said someone should teach the pirates a lesson.

Americans knew little of Europe's continual war with the Moslems and they apparently believed this propaganda, never suspecting that in the minds of the Moslems this conflict was just the latest chapter in the Crusades.

The Barbary Wars of the early 1800s were fought in and around Tripoli, which is in Libya. They were fought in the same area and over the same misunderstandings as the August 1981 air battle between U.S. and Libyan jets. Having failed to remember history, we are repeating it. We are again at war with Islam.

U.S. officials sent the Navy and Marines to attack Tripoli. European rulers watched and cheered, and I'm sure laughed up their sleeves. The U.S. government had entered the Crusades on the side of the Europeans.

The Barbary Wars were the first time American troops were hoodwinked into fighting the Europeans' wars for them, but it wouldn't be the last. In 1815 the enemy was "pirates" — now they are "terrorists," but the conflict remains the same that it's been for a thousand years, the Crusades. It was started by European rulers who conned us into becoming their allies against the Moslems.

> *"The great rule of conduct for us, in regard to foreign nations, is, in extending our commercial relations, to have with them as little political connection as possible."*
>
> George Washington, 1796

Chris, I think you can see now why George Washington's FAREWELL ADDRESS is so important. Here is part of it again:

..."a passionate attachment of one nation for another produces a variety of evils. Sympathy for the favorite nation, facilitating the illusion of an imaginary common interest in cases where no real common interest exists, and infusion into one the enmities of the other, betrays the former into a participation in the quarrels and wars of the latter, without adequate inducement or justification."

Unfortunately, foreign policy is one area where the American founders were a lot better at the theory than the application. The American republic had hardly emerged from its cradle when it gave up its neutrality and sided with the Europeans against the Moslems on "the shores of Tripoli." We have been in that Thousand Year War ever since.

Uncle Eric

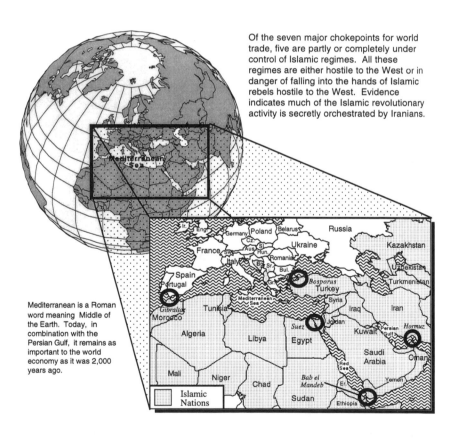

Of the seven major chokepoints for world trade, five are partly or completely under control of Islamic regimes. All these regimes are either hostile to the West or in danger of falling into the hands of Islamic rebels hostile to the West. Evidence indicates much of the Islamic revolutionary activity is secretly orchestrated by Iranians.

Mediterranean is a Roman word meaning Middle of the Earth. Today, in combination with the Persian Gulf, it remains as important to the world economy as it was 2,000 years ago.

11

The Ruling Gangs

Dear Chris,

Maps of the Islamic nations show borders and names of countries, but these borders and countries do not really exist. The borders are mere lines drawn in the sand by European rulers when they were carving up the Mideast into their various empires. The people who live there had nothing to do with creating these borders. They resent the borders and try to ignore them.

The way Europeans would keep control of their colonies was to select the most vicious tribe in each area and give this tribe whatever weapons and money it needed to subdue the others. Mass arrests, torture and executions were commonplace, and still are.

In other words, these vicious tribes, these gangsters, were established as governments by the Europeans, not by their own people. Weapons and money supplied by European rulers were used to murder thousands of innocent Moslems.

The original Algerian government was established by the French.

The original Libyan government was established by the Italians.

The Egyptian government was established by the British.
The Iranian government was established by the Russians and British.
The Syrian government was established by the French.
The Iraqi government was established by the British, and so on.

The textbook example of this process is **Saudi Arabia**. With British help, the Saudi tribe conquered four other tribes, took control of Arabia and renamed it Saudi Arabia (for further information see the Appendix). This was much like someone named Smith conquering Texas and renaming it Smith Texas. The fraud has been so successful that many westerners now say "the Saudis" when they mean anyone living in Saudi Arabia — like referring to everyone in Texas as "the Smiths." The correct term for persons living in Saudi Arabia is Arabians.

The British and French did most of this empire building in the Mideast, so they are the most hated of the Europeans.

A very important point: *People who live under these Mideast governments feel little allegiance toward them. In most cases they hate them, and they are certainly not represented by them.*

The Mideast remains mostly tribal, with the individual's loyalty belonging to his family, village and friends. In his mind, his "country" doesn't exist, it is a fiction created by European invaders.

Chris, you might want to watch the 1962 movie LAWRENCE OF ARABIA starring Peter O'Toole and Omar Sharif. It does a decent job of depicting tribal loyalty.

Sometimes the gangsters controlling these "countries" are overthrown and replaced by someone else, often by one of the paranoid maniacs the Thousand Year War has created.

Khomeini replaced the Shah in Iran. In Syria, Hafez Assad rose to power; in Iraq, Saddam Hussein.

The Saudis are so afraid of their own people that they keep two armies roughly equal in size so that if one army tries to overthrow them, the other, they hope, can be pitted against it to protect them.

They also keep their armies small so that the troops and officers can be more easily watched. This makes their armed forces too small to defend such a large country with all that oil, so the Saudis family relies on the U.S. to defend them and their oil.

The same for Kuwait and the other Gulf oil states.

U.S. officials refer to their Mideast allies as moderates but none of these Islamic governments is moderate. The most important U.S. ally (because it has so much oil) is Saudi Arabia which has no elections, no constitution and no bill of rights; no freedom of speech, religion or the press. Any American who had to live in "moderate" Saudi Arabia as the Arab natives do, without an American passport, would feel he was living in Nazi Germany.

The "moderate" government of Egypt receives more than $2 billion in U.S. foreign aid each year. Says one Egyptian woman, "Our rulers find it very easy to declare democracy during the day and arrest you at night." The victims know U.S. officials are backing this regime, so you can imagine what they think of us.

Covert operations designed to pit one tribe against another have long been a favorite tool of European rulers. Divide and conquer. This is a primary reason the Mideast remains such a violent place, European rulers spent a thousand years making it that way.

Uncle Eric

12

Rich vs. Poor

Dear Chris,

The Arab and Moslem peoples are hypersensitive about the distribution of wealth; the poor resent the rich intensely. This jealousy is due not so much to socialist attitudes, as in Europe and the U.S., but to the way the Mideast was carved up by the Europeans.

When oil was discovered in the Mideast, Europeans wanted to guarantee their access to it. They drew the national boundaries so that a small number of their puppet tribes would own and control all the black gold. The Kuwaiti and Saudi tribes are two examples.

Chris, this created extremes of wealth and poverty which are unprecedented anywhere on earth. One tribe might have so much money they cannot count it, and they've never worked a day in their lives; the neighboring tribe down the road lives in poverty and works for the wealthy tribe at minimum wages.

Because of the European desire to concentrate ownership of the oil, there are now about 10 million Arab "haves" and 250 million Arab "have nots."

Many of the haves are decadent and arrogant, and deeply hated by the have nots, who regard them as henchmen of the

West. Each morning when the have nots go to work for their overbearing employers they are reminded of the meddling of the West. The hatred grows.

Uncle Eric

The Oil Corridor

Kazakhstan

Russia

Caspian Sea

Black Sea

Aral Sea

Georgia

Uzbekistan

Armenia   Azerb.

Turkey

Turkmenistan

Syria

Iraq   **Iran**

Jordan

Kuwait

Saudi Arabia

Persian Gulf

Red Sea

U.A.E. Oman

Oil or gas field
R   Refinery
Oil Corridor

70% of the total world oil supply is in the oil corridor (shaded area). The two most angry enemies of the West — Iraq and Iran — are in the center of it. Virtually the entire area is Islamic, and battles between the West and the Islamic world have been fought here since the Middle Ages, often between Russians and Moslems. This Thousand Year War between the Islamic world and the West is common knowledge in the Mideast but almost unknown in the West.

13

Carving the World

Dear Chris,

After World War II, the U.S. and Soviet governments replaced the old European regimes as the rulers of the world, carving the globe into their two "spheres of influence," meaning their two empires. Almost every country was pressured into the choice of joining either the U.S. sphere or the Soviet sphere.

U.S. powerseekers justified their support of Batista, Diem, the Shah and their other brutal surrogates by saying they were protecting the world against the Soviet communist threat. Soviet rulers justified their support of their cutthroats by claiming they were protecting the world against the American imperialist threat.

The game worked well for powerseekers on both sides, but now the Moslems have thrown in a monkey wrench. When the Shah of Iran was overthrown in 1979, the Islamic rebels who replaced him said they would not be part of either superpower's sphere of influence, they would be independent.

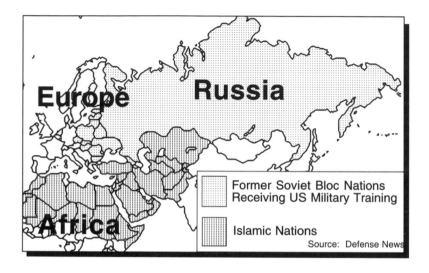

Former Soviet Bloc Nations Receiving US Military Training

Islamic Nations

Source: Defense News

Russians, Serbs and other Eastern Orthodox Christians in East Europe have fought with the Islamic world for centuries. Have U.S. officials gotten us into something they do not understand?

Chris, this was a precedent neither superpower could let stand. Both were hoping Iraqi rulers would put down the Iranian revolution, and both spent years helping the Iraqis after Saddam Hussein attacked Iran in 1980. This is why the U.S. fleet was sent into the Persian Gulf during the **Iran-Iraq war**, to help the Kuwaitis who were helping the Iraqis. (For more information on the Iran-Iraq war, see the Appendix).

But the Iraqi regime failed and the Iranian revolution against the two superpowers spread quickly. In 1989, former NBC Moscow correspondent Frank Bourgholtzer reported that Soviet officials had become concerned about the "illegal manufacture and stockpiling of weapons" including "heavy weapons" in Moslem areas of the Soviet Union.[25]

By 1992, all six Islamic states of the Soviet Union had split and declared independence. The Kremlin was afraid to try to stop them.

In 1994, the Chechens, who are Moslem, declared independence from Russia, kicking off the Chechen war, which the Chechens won.

> "The United States never really had an Iraq policy. It had an Iran policy.... Saddam's frontal assault on America's worst enemy [Iran] was like an answer to our prayers. ... Washington had groped its way toward a well-defined policy construct of helping one thuggish regime against another thuggish regime."[26]
>
> THE ARABISTS
> by Robert D. Kaplan

It is likely we have not seen the last of the battles between Moslems and Russians, who are Eastern Orthodox Christian and one of the Islamic world's oldest and most hated enemies.

Uncle Eric

---

[25] "Letter From Moscow" by Frank Bourgholtzer, SACRAMENTO BEE FORUM, April 2, 1989

[26] THE ARABISTS by Robert D. Kaplan, The Free Press, New York, 1993, p.263, 266

W. EUROPE

Catholics
&
Protestants

Croats

Balkans

E. EUROPE

Eastern
Orthodox
Christians

Serbs

Moslems

ISLAMIC WORLD

Russia's heritage is Eastern Orthodox Christian, as is Serbia's. Russians and Serbs have fought Moslems for centuries, the Turkish Ottoman Empire was their most hated enemy. Turkic homelands in central Asia ("Turkistan") were not well protected by the Ottoman Empire and were finally conquered and absorbed into the USSR in the 1920s and '30s. Main battlegrounds in the many wars between Russia and Turkey were the Caucasus Mountain area between Turkey and Russia, where Chechnya is, and the Balkans where Bosnia and Kosovo are.

14

U.S. Aid to Soviets

Dear Chris,

In the early 1980's when Ronald Reagan entered office we were continually warned about the Soviet threat. Mr. Reagan reminded us over and over about the "evil empire" and the millions of innocent Russians who had been murdered and enslaved by Soviet officials.

Then, by the time Mr. Reagan left office, the public image of the evil empire had been transformed. Gorbachev was a "nice guy." Soviet rulers were "fine people" and they deserved more loans and other assistance from the West.

What happened?

The Iraqi regime failed to put down Iran's Islamic revolution.

We cannot know what U.S. and Soviet rulers were thinking when the Iran-Iraq war ended in 1988, but my guess is they were so frightened that they climbed into bed with each other to join forces against the Islamic comeback.

The main weakness in the superpower game of dividing up the world was that the Union of Soviet Socialist Republics was exactly what its name said, socialist. Its economy did not work.

The Moscow regime survived only through aid from the U.S. and its NATO allies. In 1988, the WALL STREET JOURNAL found that the U.S. government and its allies and banks controlled by them had been loaning money to the Soviet bloc at the rate of $700 million per month; total loans had surpassed $130 billion.

By the time the Soviet empire had splintered in 1991, western "loans" were flowing in at the rate of two billion per month, but even this could not stop the collapse.

And, these were not loans, they were gifts. No one who understood socialism believed one nickel of the $130 billion could ever be repaid, and it never was.

Further, the $130 billion was paltry compared to the aid in the form of goods and services. If you'd like a thoroughly documented list of the factories, aircraft designs, computers, ships and other kinds of U.S. aid that propped up the Soviet tyranny, read Antony Sutton's fine book THE BEST ENEMY MONEY CAN BUY.

Chris, Moscow rulers were frightened. They had a socialist economy that did not work and a Moslem enemy trying to shatter their empire. Worse, they had lost the war in Afghanistan, which demonstrated that Moslem guerrillas could beat the Soviet army.

Kremlin bosses knew that they had to get more help from the U.S. and its allies or they would go under.

But, the U.S. and its allies were in a recession and were apparently unable to bail them out.

By 1992, the Soviet empire had fallen like a house of cards in a stiff wind, and for the first time everyone could see that the Islamic threat was real and serious.

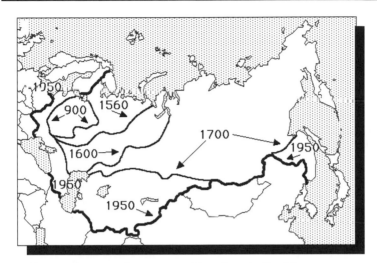

About a thousand years ago Russians in the Moscow area began conquering groups around them, gradually expanding their empire. The Russians' last thrust southward was the 1979 invasion of Afghanistan. This ended in defeat in February 1989 after Afghan tribesmen acquired shoulder-launched guided missiles. Nine months later the whole Russian empire began to break up as Russian troops refused to attack rebels. In hopes of stopping the disintegration, the Kremlin drew the line in Chechnya in 1994, but the Chechens won.

After the collapse of the Soviet empire, the socialist taxes, regulations and welfare programs were retained, so the economies could not recover.

President Bill Clinton and Vice President Al Gore led a massive effort to persuade western investors to pour money into Russia. By October 1998, another $200 billion in western money, both public and private, had disappeared into that black hole,[27] but socialist Russia continued to decline.

---

[27] Wall Street Journal, September 1, 1998, p.A19.

Europe's ancient front-line defense against the Islamic world — Russia — had dried up and blown away. (For more on Russia, see the Appendix.)

What comes next? It's hard to say, but we do know it will not likely be peace and prosperity.

Uncle Eric

15

The Invincible Secret Weapon

Dear Chris,

For a half century the U.S. armed forces have been the most powerful ever known. Yet, during the 1960s and '70s, they were beaten by rice farmers armed mostly with light shoulder weapons.

In 1994, in Somalia, they were again beaten, by small bands armed mostly with shoulder weapons.

For a half century the Russian armed forces have been the second most powerful ever known. In the 1980s they were beaten by primitive Afghan tribesmen armed mostly with shoulder weapons. In 1996 they were beaten again, by small bands of Chechens with shoulder weapons.

Rag-tag groups of rebels have discovered a secret weapon that strikes fear into the heart of every modern army. The Pentagon is terrified of it, but never speaks openly about it, so the American public remains in the dark.

The weapon is unstoppable, the U.S. has no way to counter it.

I have been writing about this weapon for 15 years, Chris, but have never done a complete explanation. Now is a good time. This will be a long letter, so find a comfortable chair. Here's the story.

In any war, the big problem to solve is not invasion, it is occupation. Invasion is easy. The real problem is, once you are in, how do you stay in? Ask anyone who was on Omaha Beach in 1944. Getting there was easy, it was staying there that was the problem.

And, staying there is the only way to win. If troops invade and conquer, and then leave, the enemy just starts over. In 1996, the U.S. fired 47 cruise missiles at Iraq. All the targets were immediately rebuilt or replaced.[28] The missiles cost $1 million each.

Troops must occupy the territory, destroy the government and wipe out any resistance, including anyone suspected of helping the resistance.

Resistance means guerrillas. The secret weapon the Pentagon refuses to discuss is guerrilla warfare.

Guerrillas prevent occupation.

Chris, a guerrilla is not a uniformed soldier who lives in a barracks and follows orders from a central command. He is a farmer, merchant or taxi driver by day, and a free lance sniper or saboteur by night.

The guerrilla operates on the very simple principle that a soldier cannot shoot what he cannot find.

The guerrilla is not much interested in killing privates or corporals, unless he can get a lot of them; he wants colonels and generals. And, he has no intentions of making his move unless he can do it and slip quietly away. His wife and children are nearby.

How does he do this? Here's one scenario: In the woods near an enemy base he places a mortar in a hole. He aims the mortar at the enemy's headquarters or barracks, then fills in

---

[28] NAVY TIMES, February 9, 1998, p.11

the hole so that the muzzle of the mortar is exactly level with the ground. He places a flat rock over the muzzle, scatters some leaves for camouflage, then goes home.

On a dark, rainy night a few months later, he slips out of bed and returns to the flat rock. He removes the rock and quickly drops in six mortar rounds, replaces the rock and runs. Next morning he is back at work driving his cab.

A few months later, he does it again, then again and again.

That's guerrilla war. The hit-and-run motif is limited only by the imagination of the guerrilla.

Guerrillas can be especially creative about booby traps. They also like sniper rifles, and in recent years have acquired small anti-tank and anti-aircraft missiles, which the Chechens and Afghans used to such good effect against the Russians.

I'm afraid, Chris, it gets worse. Every Vietnam veteran knows that even a ten-year old child can hand a soldier a Coke can with a grenade inside.

And, even those individuals who aren't directly fighting the enemy, might be aiding a guerrilla who is.

The Balkan peninsula, which is a maze of forested mountains, is ideal for guerrilla warfare. Its roads are nearly impassable for tanks, its miserable weather often makes air support impossible, and its dozens of hostile ethnic groups loath outsiders and each other.

The grudges harbored by these groups are totally unfathomable to Americans. Each village is a separate country with its own heroes, allies, loves and hates. Mostly hates. You never know who is shooting at you or why, you know only that they are probably trying to dupe you into retaliating against their enemies in the next village.

Europe is the most violent part of the world.

A small area, Europe (including Russia west of the Urals) is only 6.6% of the earth's land area, but thanks to its Roman heritage it has given us all the worst wars in history. Some of the most terrible have been the wars between Moslems and Europe's three main Christian groups — Catholics, Protestants and Eastern Orthodox Christians. The Balkan Penninsula has been the most violent part of Europe since the Middle Ages, this has been the frontline battlefield between Christians and Moslems. Anyone who gets involved in a Balkan war is courting disaster. In addition to death and destruction, it is likely to bring massive changes in flows of money and in the investment markets.

The Balkans are the most violent part of Europe.

Government is comprised of human beings, and it is the only institution that has the legal privilege of taking money by force. This privilege is called taxation. It violates the rule "Thou shalt not steal." Religions have differing opinions as to why government should have this privilege. They also have differing guidelines about who should be taxed and to what extent. When taxes are low, religious differences are unimportant, but when a government is voracious for taxes these differences can lead to war. In regions where religious opinions differ widely and taxes are high, war is nearly inevitable. The Balkan peninsula is probably the most dangerous place on earth.

Balkan Nation	Percentages			
	Catholic	Protestant	Orthodox	Moslem
Slovenia	96	N	2	1
Hungary	67	25	N	N
Romania	3	6	73	N
Croatia	76	L	11	1
Bosnia	15	4	31	40
Serbia	4	1	65	19
Bulgaria	L	L	85	13
Macedonia	N	N	59	26
Albania	10	L	20	70
Greece	L	L	98	1
Turkey	L	L	L	99

N=Not available
L=Less than 1%

Ed Vulliamy of the London GUARDIAN traveled in Bosnia. One man told him, "Vukasin Stankovic burned my house. He was my next-door neighbor, my friend; he used to come over for coffee." Another said, "Something deep in my brain says I must return one day both to take my daughter home and to find the men who did this. I know exactly who they are. They were our neighbors." Will these people obey a peace agreement?

If President Clinton's Balkan peace plan works, it will be the luckiest long shot in all world history. In attempting to pacify the Balkans, he is trying to do what nine German divisions in World War II could not do. Some of Germany's best, these units were cut to ribbons in guerrilla ambushes by groups they knew nothing about.

> "I am satisfied that the NATO implementation plan is clear, limited and achievable; and that the risks to our troops are minimized."
>
> Bill Clinton, 11/21/95

Hitler's war machine was heavily dependent on the oil fields at Ploesti in Romania. The Allies needed to destroy this oil supply. They had already invaded the Italian peninsula, but after the Germans' Balkan thrashing they were so afraid to put troops on the Balkan peninsula that they launched the infamous Ploesti air raid. Of the 178 B-24s sent on this extreme long-range mission, 54 went down, and only 33 came back in airworthy condition. The raid was so awful it turned out to be the most decorated military mission in all U.S. history; it yielded five Medals of Honor.

The raid was only partly effective, so, despite the horrific losses, the Allies continued the bombing for another year. The total cost mounted, until it was a staggering 350 planes and 2,800 men, yet the U.S. and Britain steadfastly refused to use ground troops to take the critically important Ploesti oil fields.

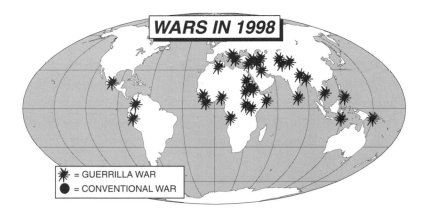

Wars are spreading, and all of them are guerrilla wars. The last conventional war was fought in Iraq in 1991.

If George Patton or Irwin Rommel were here today we'd have no doubt what they would say about President Clinton putting U.S. troops in the Balkans. But, of course, Mr. Clinton's military prowess is far greater than theirs.

How long will President Clinton's crusade last? In 1996 Mr. Clinton said the troops would be out in one year. The president of France said decades.

Keep an eye on the Balkan weather. Any day of bad flying weather is a day when U.S. troops are most vulnerable to ambush.

The point is, where guerrilla activities occur, a soldier does not know who can be trusted, because he does not know who the guerrillas are. In his mind, the only way to be absolutely certain of the enemy, is to kill everyone, which is unconscionable.

Chris, the Pentagon's big secret is that an occupation army must be a very different animal than an invasion army.

An invasion requires well equipped expert warriors who can punch through the enemy's defenses and establish bases for the occupation.

The occupation requires an army of cold-blooded homicidal maniacs.[29]

American soldiers had no trouble getting into Vietnam. It was staying there and remaining honorable that was virtually impossible.

Soldiers commanded by Lt. William Calley in Vietnam had been taking casualties day after day without even seeing the enemy, much less getting a chance to shoot back. They finally snapped, attacking and burning the village of My Lai. Some 500 men, women and children were massacred.

Chris, Americans lose guerrilla wars because we no longer have the stomach for mass murder. After My Lai, Lieutenant Calley was court martialed.

My Lai was not the only incident of this kind. In August 1965, three marines were wounded outside Da Nang. When their buddies arrived at a nearby village, they tore the place apart, then burned it, at one point threatening to use a flame-thrower on a ditch full of cowering women and children.

---

[29] Assuming the enemy resists. In 1945, Germans and Japanese did not. In history, non-resistance is the exception, not the rule.

When news footage of this incident ran on television, the network received a flood of angry phone calls. But viewers were not protesting that the troops behaved badly, they were protesting that the incident must have been faked because American troops would never do such a horrible thing.[30]

Six decades earlier, during the U.S. conquest of the Philippines, the troops were faced with the same problem — now that we are here, how do we tell the guerrillas from the peaceful farmers, merchants and taxi drivers?

They finally gave up trying. General Jacob Smith told them, "I want no prisoners. I wish you to burn and kill; the more you burn and kill, the better it will please me."[31]

Some 220,000 Filipino men, women and children were slaughtered.[32]

Smith was court martialed.

Again, guerrilla warfare boils down to the iron law that you cannot shoot what you cannot find. The only way to kill guerrillas is to kill everyone, and Americans who do this have trouble living with themselves, or with anyone else. This, I think, explains much of the so-called Vietnam delayed stress syndrome. A lot of GIs did things they aren't proud of, and they don't know enough about real politics to understand what happened to them.

When a soldier fights guerrillas, he doesn't get to be John Wayne leading the cavalry over the hill to rescue the women and children. He gets to be the thug who is terrorizing the

---

[30] TV GUIDE, May 6, 1989, p.8

[31] ALMANAC OF AMERICA'S WARS by John S. Bowman, Brompton Books, Hong Kong, 1990, p. 101

[32] WALL STREET JOURNAL, "Death Toll," Nov. 19, 1997, p.1

women and children. Not good for morale. I can think of nothing more Satanic than sending good men to fight guerrillas.

One of the great misconceptions about U.S. military policy is that the Pentagon and White House are afraid of getting "bogged down" in another Vietnam.

They are not afraid of getting bogged down, they are afraid of giving the order that would prevent getting bogged down. This order is the one General Smith gave in the Philippines, but no one would give in Vietnam: kill them all. Americans, with their belief in ethics, would rather give any order than that one.

The result is mass confusion. As I mentioned in an earlier letter, in a post-war survey of 108 Army generals who had served in Vietnam, 70% said U.S. objectives were not clear, and 52% said the stated objectives could not be achieved.[33]

Of course, the objective of victory could have been achieved, but only by killing every Vietnamese, and the court martial of Lt. Calley had shown that mass murder would not be condoned.

Army War College instructor Colonel Harry G. Summers once talked with a former North Vietnamese colonel. "You know," said Summers, "you never defeated us on the battlefield." The Vietnamese replied, "That may be so, but it is also irrelevant."[34]

Against guerrillas, firepower is not much help. Historian Lawrence Engelmann tells the story about Richard Nixon calling a meeting of war experts after he was elected in 1969. Nixon requested a comparison of the military and economic

---

[33] WALL STREET JOURNAL, January 14, 1985, p.8
[34] VIETNAM, by Stanley Karnow, published by Viking Press, NY, 1983, p.17

resources available to the U.S. and North Vietnam, and a projected date for the U.S. to win the war. Engelmann says all this was fed into a computer, which cranked out the answer: "U.S. wins in 1965."[35]

In Vietnam, a nation smaller than California, U.S. aircraft dropped more than three times the tonnage of bombs that were dropped in all theaters of World War II. It worked out to 1,000 pounds of explosives for each man, woman and child in the country.[36]

Summarizing, the only reliable way to win a guerrilla war is to use **ethnic cleansing**. If you are not evil enough to do this, you lose.

In Somalia, U.S. troops would not do it. They lost.

This is a main reason U.S. troops are in 144 countries now. That's about two-thirds of all the countries on earth.[37] They train foreign troops to do the anti-guerrilla dirty work that Washington will not do.

This training is one of the main reasons so many millions of foreigners hate the U.S.

Chris, anyone who thinks the spread of guerrilla war will not cause radical changes in the world economy and investment markets is living in a fool's paradise. This is major historical shift but no one talks about it because the Pentagon pretends it isn't happening.

A key point the Pentagon will not discuss is that almost always, guerrilla troops are defensive not offensive. Civilians by day, they are mostly amateurs operating alone or in small groups. It is nearly impossible to induce them to leave home and family to invade someone else's country.

---

[35] SACRAMENTO BEE FORUM, April 30, 1995, p.1
[36] "Myths About Vietnam's Fall," by Larry Engelmann, Sacramento Bee Forum, April 30, 1995, p.1.
[37] AIR FORCE TIMES, August 3, 1998, p.31.

This means that, in nearly every case, if you find yourself fighting a guerrilla, you are on the wrong side. He is not in your country, you are in his.

In response to the My Lai massacre, officers and NCOs today are required to take courses in ethics, most of which are taught by chaplains.

This prohibition on murdering defenseless civilians means the U.S. cannot win a guerrilla war, because it is rarely possible to separate guerrillas from civilians. One example is the American Revolution. The British couldn't tell a minuteman from a disinterested farmer or merchant, and British officers would not wipe out whole towns, so they lost the war.

By contrast, the wars against the native Americans ended in victory because whites of European origin were willing to practice mass murder against dark-skinned natives.

Chris, another reason the U.S. cannot beat guerrillas is arithmetic. The rule of thumb among military experts is that conventional troops need a minimum six-to-one numerical superiority over guerrillas. Some would say ten-to-one, in addition to helicopters and all the other technological advantages.

I learned this 30 years ago. In the 605th Air Commando Squadron our job was anti-guerrilla warfare, politely called counter-insurgency warfare. We helped train a lot of foreign troops. We worked with the CIA's notorious School of the Americas which cultivated the likes of **Manuel Noriega**. Washington's use of U.S. troops to train foreign thugs is probably even more common now than it was then. Again, this is a big reason millions hate America.

The experience taught me that guerrillas have a tremendous advantage over regular troops. They know the terrain, can choose their time and place to strike, and rarely do strike unless they are sure they can escape.

Using air power over Vietnam, it took three B-52 bombers and 80 tons of bombs to kill one enemy. This one enemy needed nothing more than a $300 sniper rifle to keep a whole battalion of Marines tied up for days.

Hanoi calculated that if they could get just twenty supply trucks of ammunition and supplies per day through to the guerrillas in the South, the U.S. could not win the war despite all its aircraft carriers, bombers, tanks and artillery. They were right.

This, incidentally, is why the Second Amendment was included in the UNITED STATES CONSTITUTION. "A well regulated militia, being necessary for the security of a free state..." it says. Militias are civilian soldiers who can fight as guerrillas. The American founders knew that the most effective defense is one that focuses on making the country difficult to occupy. The founders believed a well trained and equipped militia does this superbly.

In the invasion of Normandy, General Eisenhower estimated that 2,800 French guerrillas trained by three OSS agents were worth 15 infantry divisions. A division is 5,000 to 10,000 troops.

In 1998, the Turkish government had 200,000 regular troops committed to fighting 1,200 Kurdish guerrillas. (For more about Kurdistan, see the Appendix.)

Back when the Second Amendment was taken seriously, the effectiveness of militia-guerrillas was understood. Lincoln once remarked that all the armies of Europe, Asia and Africa combined, with Napoleon as their commander, could not make a track on the Blue Ridge or take a drink from the Ohio.

The greatest strength of guerrillas is that they are private troops not government troops. Fighting covertly as individuals or in small groups, they must be found and destroyed one by one, for they have no central authority on which to concentrate forces to compel a surrender.

The mighty Russian army was defeated in Afghanistan and Chechnya because it had no pivotal target at which to aim its firepower, just thousands of dispersed and concealed snipers and saboteurs. It was like an elephant attacking an anthill. The elephant kills a lot of ants, but in the long run, bitten thousands of times in sensitive areas, he flees.

How do you conquer an anthill? With insecticide. Poison gas. That's how some governments fight guerrillas, and it does work, because it kills the whole population. Including the children. This is why the U.S. won't use it.

Chris, prior to Desert Storm, the Bush administration referred to Saddam Hussein as the new Hitler. They accused him of trying to dominate the world, and spoke of war crimes trials.

The orders given to the troops turned out mysteriously different. These referred only to removing Iraqi forces from Kuwait. The idea of going into central Iraq to remove this new Hitler had somehow vanished.

Why? I think it was the threat of guerrilla war.

Before the war began, General Schwartzkopf tipped his hand about the U.S. weakness toward guerrilla war. In a September 1990 interview with U.S. NEWS & WORLD REPORT, Schwartzkopf admitted, "If someone said, 'Go in and machine-gun a thousand civilians,' I'd say, 'Absolutely not!' Sorry, but I consider that illegal and immoral and I'm not going to do it."

After the fighting ended in 1991, officials revealed that the battle plan had been laid out to keep U.S. troops away from populated areas to avoid house-to-house fighting and civilian casualties. U.S. troops were to fight only in the empty desert.

Saddam Hussein was known to be an avid student of the Vietnam War, and I believe he had a two-part plan. Part one would be the set up for part two which would be an endless guerrilla war in Iraq's cities, farmlands, mountains and swamps.

The part one set up was to make Kuwait a killing ground where the West would slaughter tens of thousands of Moslem troops and trigger outrage throughout the Moslem world. In this Saddam Hussein nearly succeeded.

First he stripped Kuwait of everything valuable, including the windows and plumbing, then filled it with poorly trained slave soldiers who were held in place by the elite Republican Guards. The U.S. slaughtered these slave soldiers just as Hussein planned. One U.S. pilot called it a "turkey shoot" as 100,000 Iraqis were massacred.

Week after week the carnage dragged on, and the Moslem world began to rise up. If the slaughter had continued much longer, Mr. Bush's Arab "allies" probably would have had to switch sides or be assassinated by their own people. The next world war would have begun right there. Despite bribes to join the U.S., only 12 of the 21 Arab governments had lined up against Iraq, and many of these were wavering.

King Hassan of Morocco would likely have been the first of the 12 to go over to Saddam. He backed George Bush but his people were overwhelmingly pro-Iraq. In a February 1991 rally, 300,000 turned out. King Hassan began to speak of Saddam as his "dear Arab brother."

As U.S. forces rolled north, and the need for the occupation began, I think President Bush lost his nerve. He withdrew before the guerrilla war could begin.

Evidence supports this. After the war the Senate Armed Services Committee asked General Schwartzkopf why U.S.

forces didn't go into central Iraq to eliminate the Iraqi regime. Schwartzkopf gave two reasons: (1) the UN hadn't called for it and (2) it would have been a "tarpit" for U.S. forces. Colin Powell has used the same word, tarpit.

Chris, U.S. military policy today can be boiled down into four words: attack but don't occupy.

Because of the fear of guerrilla war, the U.S. withdrew from Iraq and left Saddam Hussein in power. Hussein, Qadaffi, Assad, Khameini and all the other New Axis enemies of the White House understand this. The Iraq-Kuwait war exposed America's **Achilles heel** — guerrilla war.

This is why I am so certain the U.S. should declare neutrality and get out of Chaostan (For more information about Chaostan, see the Appendix). The fact that the power junkies in Washington will not do so is why I am also certain we are headed for another war we will lose.

As I write this in 1999, all wars are guerrilla wars, it's what works. One of the few forecasts about which I am highly confident is that in any case where the U.S. faces guerrillas, the Pentagon and White House will run like scared rabbits, as they did in Somalia.

I believe all the weapons and tactics of the New Axis which appear to be for conventional war are really for the purpose of baiting the U.S. into a guerrilla war. The U.S. can beat anything they have except guerrillas.

Chris, It looks to me like the New Axis strategy will be a one-two punch. The first punch will be conventional war to lure in the U.S. Then will come the haymaker, an endless guerrilla war. They know the U.S. will always run from this haymaker.

So, U.S. armed forces are more than adequate to defend the American homeland, but as a global enforcer for the **United Nations** they are a **paper tiger**.

I do suspect that some in the Pentagon have begun facing this fact. Retired Lt. Col. Ralph Peters warns,

"The new century will be one of street fighting, uncontrollable masses, shortage, disease and immeasurable hatreds — all concentrated in the decaying urban landscapes in the world's least-successful states and regions. It is a kind of warfare for which our Army is unprepared. Worse, it is the type of warfare for which our Army refuses to prepare. ... It is a combat environment in which we cannot even identify our enemies."[38]

This hidden weakness of the U.S. armed forces means the entire world political and economic structure is built on sand.

Chaostan is a third of all the land on earth and it supplies a vast portion of all raw materials. Raw materials are used in virtually everything.

This means all prices today, including the prices of investments, and interest rates, are based on the assumption the U.S. armed forces will be able to prevent "rogue states" and "terrorists" from grabbing the oil and other raw materials.

Wrong. "Scramble for Oil in Central Asia Hits Roadblocks," is the headline of a WALL STREET JOURNAL article about the threat of guerrillas to the raw materials supply lines. Extraction does not equal transport. The article gives evidence that the ability to get the oil or other raw material out of the ground is not the same as the ability to get them out of Chaostan.

---

[38] Army Times, May 11, 1998, p.34

The problem is not so much economic as it is military. How do you protect the supply lines?

   Chris, these transport routes — for personnel and equipment going in as well as the product coming out — must be militarily defensible, and few in Chaostan are, because of guerrillas.

Ringed by oil fields, the Caspian is a huge prize. But it is also ringed by warring groups of guerrillas. How can the oil be transported to nations that have the money to buy it?

For instance, important oil pipelines stretch from the Caspian Sea through Azerbaijan to the Black Sea. Armenian guerrillas are a constant threat to these lines.

Try to imagine the cost of guarding thousands of miles of pipelines, rail lines and roads against attacks by hundreds of local groups, each of whom feels they should get a cut of anything traveling through their territory.

Total guerrilla-imposed taxes on each truckload of goods crossing tiny Georgia is $1,500.[39]

The key point is that prices of all raw materials coming out of Chaostan are presently based on the assumption the supply lines will remain secure and the raw materials will continue coming to market. They won't, or at least they won't at present prices. In the face of guerrillas, the forces of the U.S. and NATO are all bluff.

But, the Pentagon won't talk about guerrillas, so investors haven't a clue.

The next decade will be most interesting. Warn everyone you care about, Chris. In my next letter I want to tell you about a most amazing mystery.

Uncle Eric

---

[39] WALL STREET JOURNAL, March 3, 1998, p.A14

16

Amazing Mystery

Dear Chris,

I collect strange mysteries. It's fun and it teaches mental discipline. One learns to live with not knowing answers, to avoid the temptation of jumping to conclusions. Here is one of my favorite mysteries.

When observing world politics the tendency is to focus on countries and their borders but in Asia this is misleading. Today's countries and borders are tenuous and nearly irrelevant. The real, lasting divisions in Asia are cultural, meaning mostly religious and linguistic.

The map on the next page shows the rough boundaries of Asia's six ancient enemy cultures.

These six enemy cultures, not countries, are likely to be the strongest influence on your investments for the next decade or more. To see one reason why, notice the map also shows main oil fields.

No one knows how much oil is over there. The Tengiz, Azerbaijan and Tarim fields are big but haven't been explored enough to reveal exactly how big. They are known to be in the same league as fields in the Persian Gulf, so we can safely say the main oil areas of Asia contain somewhere between 75% and 95% of the total world oil supply.

The shocker is the locations. Nearly all of that oil is under the ancient frontiers between enemy cultures.

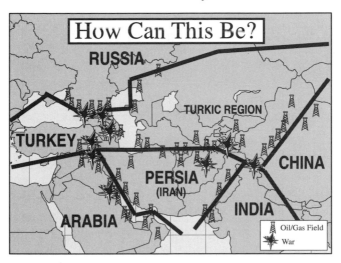

Countless wars have been fought on these frontiers, whose people hate and fear each other with a ferocity Americans experience only in their nightmares.

In short, the oil fields are the same as the ancient battle-fields. Amazing, what are the odds?

It's almost as if, were you to play connect-the-dots with the oil fields, you'd draw the ancient boundaries.

These cultural divisions were formed centuries before oil was valuable. Until kerosene was patented in 1852, oil was only a gooey, smelly nuisance. The civilizations are ancient, all go back more than a thousand years.

So, how can this be? How can most of the world's most important oil fields be under the world's oldest, most dangerous frontiers? It's nearly impossible to believe, but there it is.

Chris, if you have an explanation please write me.

Uncle Eric

17

The Israeli Tragedy

Dear Chris,

Much has been written about the so-called Arab-Israeli conflict but I do not believe it is a complex subject.

At the end of World War II a group of desperate, demoralized Jews were looking for a safe place to call home and they chose Palestine. I doubt any of them had the slightest idea they were walking into the heart of a ten-century war.

Most of these new Jewish arrivals in Palestine were Europeans. When they began helping to create a Jewish state in Palestine, the Arab-Moslem **Palestinians** saw this as a repeat of the creation of the Crusader states. Remember the castles.

Two of the three main divisions of the Palestine Liberation Organization (PLO) are named after battles fought during the Crusades.

Some Jews today are still mystified at the depth of the hatred aimed at them. They do not realize they've blundered into a feud they had no part in starting. The Crusades have always been between European rulers and Moslems, Jews played little part until this century.

Indeed, Jews and Moslems are the two most persecuted peoples on earth. Both have suffered terribly at the hands of

European rulers. They should be closest friends and I am convinced they still could be if foreign governments would withdraw from the Mideast and stop meddling in Mideast affairs.

In fact, I'd like to see Jews and Moslems uniting in a coalition to tell all foreign governments to get out of the Mideast and stay out. If European Jews had understood Moslem history in 1948, I am sure this is what would have happened, and maybe it still will, but don't count on it. Feelings now are so intense that it is nearly impossible to discuss the Arab-Israeli conflict without being shouted down or beaten senseless.

Incidentally, do not confuse **Judaism** with **Zionism**. Judaism is the Jewish religion. Zionism is a political movement intended to create a Jewish state.

Some Jews are Zionists, others are not.

Most Moslem hatred is directed at Zionists, not Jews generally, although as the war intensifies this distinction is being lost.

The Moslem rector of al-Azhar University once said, "We religious leaders have also to make clear to the Islamic peoples that the lingering spirit of the past Crusades that was utterly routed by the feats of valor and heroic resistance of our forefathers has made of the present-day Zionism a spearhead launched against Muslims by the enemies of humanity and advocates of imperialism."[40]

Chris, "feats of valor" was a reference to the great Moslem leader Saladin, who threw the Europeans out of the Holy Land during the Middle Ages.

Uncle Eric

---

[40] THE DAGGER OF ISLAM by John Laffin, Bantam Books, 1981, p.58

F8U Crusader

Few Americans have any understanding of what Europeans have done to Moslems, or how Moslems feel about it. This can be seen in the fact the the F8U jet fighter carried on U.S. aircraft carriers (and French carriers) for more than 30 years was named the Crusader. This slap in the face to Moslems was probably not deliberate, most likely the name Crusader was chosen simply because Americans did not know.

The above illustration is a black and white rendering of the F8U jet fighter used on the cover of this book.

18

Playing One Against The Other

Dear Chris,

For several years before the 1989 Soviet withdrawal from
Afghanistan, thousands of Arab Moslems from other Mideast countries went into Afghanistan to join the fight. Their
battle cry was, "Death to America, Death to the Soviets,
Death to the Israelis!"[41]
In it's present form the war is essentially an Islamic
rebellion against the U.S. and Russia, and secondarily against
other European powers and Israel. But this is hidden by the
fact that some Moslem groups form alliances with the U.S.
or Russia, and sometimes even with Israelis whenever it
suits their purposes. In other words, they play the western
regimes against each other.
Afghans accepted help from the U.S. to conquer the
Soviets. Iranians occasionally become friendly with Russians to counter the U.S. Egyptian rulers were once in the
Soviet sphere of influence but U.S. officials pay better and
now they are in the U.S. sphere.
Moslem rebels would like to throw all foreign governments out of their homelands — this is what the war is about.
They don't mind having trade and commerce with us but
they don't want our governments meddling in their affairs.
Do they want our foreign aid money?

[41] MacNeil Lehrer News Hour, March 28, 1989

Chris, it is crucially important to remember that the Islamic governments are not the Islamic people. The governments get most of the money, and they are brutal. If you don't believe they are brutal, go to the U.S. State Department's web site for travelers[42] and read what the travel advisories say about these countries. As you read about, say, Saudi Arabia, remember that this is the U.S. government's own web site talking about its own *allies*.

And, remember that it wasn't so long ago that U.S. officials were allied with Saddam Hussein. He was fighting Iran, so he was a good guy, right?

U.S. aid money goes mostly to the governments not the people, which means the money is used to oppress the Islamic people.

As you read the State Department's warnings about traveling in these nations, try to imagine what it would be like to live there. As I said in an earlier letter, most of the world is like that. If being born in America were the only good thing that ever happened to me, I would nevertheless be astoundingly lucky.

An ancient Islamic tradition concerns the **Mahdi** (The Guided One), a hero who will come from God to unite Moslems against their enemies. I am wondering if a Mahdi will emerge from Afghanistan. The Afghans conquered the Russians, and no one has done that since...when? Has anyone ever done it?

Yes, the Mongols. In 1240.

And the Moslem Chechens in 1996.

Chris, many Moslem leaders attribute their victories to Allah. Powerful stuff. I'll go into more detail in my next letter.

Uncle Eric

---

[42] At the time of this writing the URL is http://travel.state.gov/travel_warnings.html

19

The Coming Messiahs

Dear Chris,

I'd like to explain more about the Mahdi.

The U.S. "victory" in the Iraq-Kuwait war has created the most extreme example of overconfidence since Hitler attacked the USSR. Convinced they have some kind of right to Persian Gulf oil, many Americans now believe the Islamic world is inhabited by ignorant camel jockeys who haven't a prayer of beating the mighty high-tech West.

Chris, it's not a new story. The British and French pioneered the practice of picking senseless fights with Moslems, and U.S. officials have enthusiastically adopted this tradition. No western government has ever appreciated how quickly these "primitive" people can turn into an unstoppable military force. The only missing ingredient is a charismatic leader, a Mahdi.

In the 1880s, the British thought they would have no trouble subduing Islamic rebels in Sudan. British-led Egyptian troops had steamships, rockets, the latest Remington rifles, Krupp howitzers, Nordenfelt machine guns and vast stores of ammunition. The rebels had camels, spears and swords.

The rebels also had the brilliant Mohammed Ahmed, who claimed to be the promised Mahdi.

British **hubris** led to one defeat after another, with their troops wiped out, and their superb weapons falling into the hands of the rebels. In 3 1/2 years, the rebels had taken the whole Sudan — a half-million square miles — and killed General Charles Gordon, who was the Patton of his day. The British were shocked and astounded, and the rebels held Sudan fourteen years.

The Mahdi was single-minded and direct in his purpose, while British rulers played politics, repeatedly sending their troops to die for no logical reason.

Chris, I see the British experience in the Sudan as a precedent for the oil-rich Persian Gulf during the new century.

The U.S. government and its pet oil dictators are making the same mistakes the British made in Sudan, and I think they will get thrown out of the Persian Gulf just as the mighty British were thrown out of Sudan.

I am wondering if Iran's new "moderate" president Khatami is the man who will do it. The Mahdi claimed to be descended from Mohammed. So does Khatami.

The Mahdi legend is strongest among Shiite Moslems. Most of the population surrounding the Gulf is Shiite, and Iran is 93% Shiite.

Most Gulf oil is in the hands of U.S.-backed dictators who are Sunni, and despised by their people. These Sunni dictators rose to power with the help of the British, which is almost the worst pedigree a ruler can have in the Islamic world. (The worst is probably Russian.)

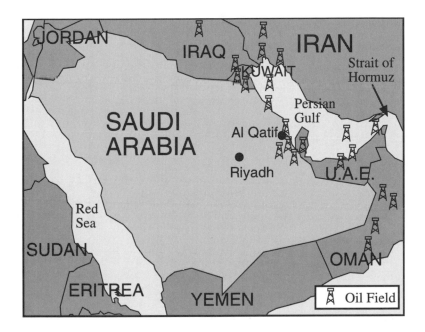

Iranians (Persians) and Arabs are ancient enemies. Iranians are mostly Shiite, Arabs are mostly Sunni.

Saudi Arabia's angry Shiite Moslem minority lives around Al Qatif in the center of the oil fields. Does Iran intend to foment a revolution here?

Interest in a Mahdi usually peaks during times of turmoil. Since the Soviet Empire began breaking up in 1989, no less than 23 wars have broken out in Chaostan.

Highly lethal modern weapons are available to anyone with the money to buy them, and during the 1990s, Iran and Iraq bought them by the trainload. Israel and the European Christian nations already had plenty.

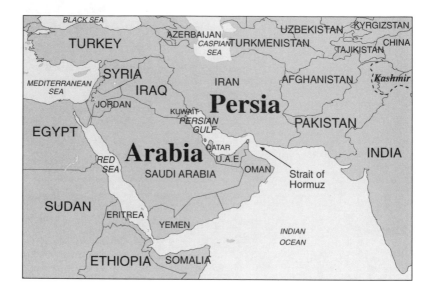

Persia (Iran) has been a heavily populated civilization for 25 centuries and has always dominated the Persian Gulf. This is why the gulf is called the Persian Gulf. Iran is Shiite. It's Sunni enemy Arabia is and always has been mostly empty desert. Arab citizens of the U.S.-backed oil dictatorships on the west side of the Gulf number no more than 25 million. Iran's population is 67.5 million, and Shiites in southern Iraq are another 13 million, for a total of more than 80 million Shiites vs. 25 million Sunnis. The military forces of the U.S.-backed dictatorships are small and poorly trained, and their loyalty to their rulers is suspect, so the only real barrier standing between the Shiites and the oil is the U.S. military, which is spread very thin. The oil will belong to Iran, the only question is when.

Not one American in a thousand, Chris, understands what is brewing in the Persian Gulf. As mentioned earlier, during the past five centuries, there has rarely been a five-year period when European troops have not been under arms on Moslem soil. The Moslems will have their revenge on the West, all they need is a capable leader.

This brings me to the 1966 movie KHARTOUM starring Charlton Heston, who plays General Gordon. It's about the final battles between the Mahdi and the British in Sudan. KHARTOUM is historically accurate in most respects, and it will give you a feel for the mess the Europeans created in the Islamic world. View it as soon as you can, then loan it and this letter to everyone you care about.

What the movie does not show is Gordon's letters expressing his opinion that Sudanese Moslems had every right to throw the British out of their homeland.[43]

As you watch, imagine the Mahdi with radio, television and the Internet to spread his message; and his troops with cruise missiles, nerve gas and possibly nuclear weapons.

I believe a big oil war is as inevitable as anything in human affairs can be. Exactly when it will start, I wish I could say. The rulers of Iraq and Iran do not keep me informed of their war plans. But I do know how they feel about us, and I know they are sitting right on top of the Persian Gulf oil fields while we are 9,000 sea miles away.

When it happens, the price of oil will skyrocket.

Uncle Eric

---

[43] PRISONERS OF THE MAHDI, by Byron Farwell, Harper & Row, 1967, p.77,82

20

The Ultimate Weapon

Dear Chris,

Government officials and military officers in every country have long wished for a weapon that would make them invincible. Bows and arrows, flintlock rifles, cannons and battleships were all heralded as ultimate weapons, but in time each was superseded by something new and even more effective.

Few realize the true ultimate weapon was invented in the Mideast nine centuries ago. It was described by Marco Polo who passed through Persia in 1273 and wrote an account of a fortress in the valley of Alamut. This fortress was the headquarters of the organization that had developed the ultimate weapon.

No one has ever found an effective defense against this weapon and top officials in every nation fear it so much they have a tacit agreement never to use it. This agreement is the oldest arms-control agreement in effect — at least, the oldest I know of — but the Moslems who invented the weapon have never subscribed to it. I believe the Moslems are taking their weapon out of the closet to use on Washington and its allies. Here's the story.

Like Christianity, Chris, Islam is splintered into numerous sects large and small. One of the smallest during the Middle Ages was a group living just south of the Caspian Sea.

This small sect was persecuted by other sects around them. One of the first attacks was led by Mu'in al-Din Kashi who gave orders "to kill them wherever they were, and wherever they were conquered to pillage their property and enslave their women."[44]

The sect built their fortress but had so few men to defend it — in one case less than a hundred — that they realized drastic measures were needed. Leaders and teachers of this sect were highly educated in science, math and technology, and they set about developing the new weapon.

One of the first targets was Sultan Sanjar. Sanjar's intended victims had sent ambassadors to request peace but Sanjar ignored them. So, one morning Sanjar awoke to find a dagger stuck in the ground beside his bed. Imagine yourself in this situation, how would you feel?

Sanjar was terrified and tried to keep the matter secret but Hasan-i Sabbah, leader of the persecuted sect, sent a message: "Did I not wish the Sultan well, that dagger which was struck into the hard ground would have been planted in his soft breast."[45] From then on the Sultan left these people alone.

The weapon Hasan-i Sabbah had used was a true-life medieval version of the "Mission Impossible" strike force we see on the TV show and movie of that name. It was a highly skilled group of specialists trained and equipped to menace the *leaders* of the attacking force and, if necessary, kill them. The leaders, only the leaders, not the troops.

---

[44] THE ASSASSINS, by Bernard Lewis, Oxford University Press, NY, 1967, p.64

[45] Ibid., p.58

How could they get close enough to kill a leader? Writing in 1332, German scholar Brocardus said the members of this Mission Impossible team were masters of disguise trained in "the gestures, garments, languages, customs and acts of various nations and peoples."[46]

Security forces could not stop them. These teams were trained to imitate and join these security forces.

Totally dedicated to their cause, these specialists would sometimes spend years planning and preparing for missions.

In one case, an envoy was sent to an enemy sultan who had been planning an attack. The envoy told the sultan that his message was to be delivered in private. He was searched, no weapons were found and the hall was cleared of all but a few people.

The envoy repeated that the information was for the sultan's ears only. The sultan dismissed all but two guards and said, "give your message." The envoy replied, "I have been ordered to deliver it in private only." The sultan declared, "These two do not leave me. If you wish, deliver your message, and if not, return."

The envoy asked, "Why do you not send away these two as you sent away the others?" The sultan explained, "I regard these as my own sons, and they and I are as one."

The envoy turned to the two guards and said, "If I ordered you in the name of the master to kill this sultan, would you do so?" Both answered yes and drew their swords, saying, "Command us as you wish." The messenger turned and left, taking the two guards with him. The sultan never bothered this sect again.[47]

---

[46] Ibid., p.1
[47] Ibid., p.116

The sultan lived, but others were not so lucky. When the Crusaders invaded, they failed to take the warnings seriously. They laid siege to the sect's fortress and tried to collect taxes from them. They also captured a member of the sect and tortured him to death.

So, on April 28, 1192, the Marquis Conrad of Montferrat, King of Jerusalem, was killed by two members of the sect's strike force. The two had been disguised as Christian monks, and they had wormed their way into the confidence of the bishop.

Chris, notice that the two killers were Moslems, yet they were so convincing as Christian monks that they could deceive a bishop.

Many enemy leaders of this sect were so afraid of them that these leaders never left their homes without wearing armor under their clothing.

When the Crusaders returned to Europe they told stories of this strange religious sect that could defeat the largest army merely by killing its leaders. Politicians were alarmed. This was unfair. Killing soldiers and civilians was a traditional and acceptable part of war, but killing politicians was definitely immoral. The practice had to be stopped before it spread.

Throughout Europe this small Moslem sect acquired a reputation for barbarism and criminality. Their style of warfare was so thoroughly abhorred that even today the name of this sect is regarded as one of the most ghastly words in the English language.

This name? The **Assassins**. Yes, this small Moslem sect was the Assassins and their weapon was **assassination**.

Today in every nation outside the Mideast this weapon is regarded as inherently evil. Killing thousands of soldiers and civilians is fair, but killing a politician is unfair and no "civilized" nation does it.

The propagandizing of the word "assassination" has been thorough. The Assassins were accused of every kind of depravity, including addiction to alcohol and narcotics, religious heresies, and rape of their own daughters, sisters and mothers.

Of course, this is not to say the Assassins were all fine fellows, they weren't; but we have no evidence they were worse than most other groups of their day. Their only important difference was that they had developed the ultimate weapon and no politician wanted this weapon used.

Nor do any today. In the U.S. it's been made illegal. Our forces can kill thousands or millions of enemy soldiers and civilians — but not one enemy leader. Killing leaders is assassination, a horrible crime.

> *"Let them know that sooner or later we shall reach the heart of the White House, the Kremlin, the Elysee and 10 Downing Street."*
>
> *Islamic Jihad spokesman*
> *July 22, 1985*

A horrible crime to us, but not in the Mideast. They invented it, they're good at it, and they see nothing wrong with it.

Interesting question: If an American politician were secretly threatened by a group of these Mideast killers, and forced to follow their orders, would he tell anyone?

Uncle Eric

21

Kill One, Create Ten More

Dear Chris,

The West's CIA and other secret agencies are amateurs compared to the followers of Mohammed. A friend who is a refugee from Iran has given me this rule of thumb about incidents in the Mideast: Whatever appears to be happening isn't what is happening, and whoever appears to be responsible isn't who is responsible.

We saw this in the 1986 attack on Libya. President Reagan claimed he had proof that someone backed by the Libyan government had instigated a bombing in Germany. After Tripoli had been hit by U.S. planes, officials acquired additional evidence that the bombing was connected not to Libya but to Syria.

So, U.S. forces were ordered to hit the wrong country and kill dozens of innocent people whose relatives and friends now have strong incentive to join the fight against us.

Each time we kill someone in the Mideast we automatically make enemies of all the relatives and friends. Killing one opponent creates ten more.

The mighty U.S. and Russian military forces are virtually useless in this war. Ships, tanks and aircraft are designed to fight each other, but they are helpless against the covert forces of Islam.

Some may be tempted to say the way to fight the war against Islam is to "nuke 'em all!" One problem. The Islamic peoples number hundreds of millions and they inhabit dozens of countries; should we nuke a large portion of the surface of the earth? Do we want to kill millions of innocent people?

And, do we want to do this when we have not yet tried the simple measure of getting out of their homelands and leaving them alone?

During the 1990s, the U.S. kept about two dozen warships in the Persian Gulf. How many Persian warships have you seen in Chesapeake Bay?

Speaking of nuclear weapons, one of the first tactics learned by the Assassins was divide and conquer. During interrogation, the Assassin killers of Italian Marquis Conrad "confessed" they had been hired not by Hasan-i Sabbah but by the King of England. This did not improve relations between Italy and England.

Today's Assassins must surely be developing ways to create incidents that will pit the U.S. and other — nuclear armed? — nations against each other.

The original Assassin strike teams were usually caught immediately after they had achieved their objectives. They were so dedicated to their cause that they would deliberately surrender and under interrogation give false information that would divide their enemies.

This willingness to undertake suicide missions may seem fanatical and irrational to us, but during war, soldiers volunteer for it. When our enemies go on suicide missions we call it lunacy; when our troops do it we call it heroism.

Chris, what will happen if someone bombs the U.S. Capitol or commits some other major terrorist act and confesses to television cameras that he was hired by China or some other nuclear-armed enemy of Washington?

What will happen if a city in China is hit and the Moslem attacker confesses he was hired by the U.S.?

Are the infiltrators already in place, ready to launch their attacks when they receive orders?

Let's look at the Islamic principle of **taqiyya** which was widely applied by the Assassins. Taqiyya is a doctrine of dispensation. Moslems are required to practice their faiths but when under duress they are permitted to conceal and disguise their beliefs. An Assassin never looked like an Assassin. Sometimes they would spend years as Christian or Jewish soldiers in the enemy's army patiently waiting for the day when they received orders to kill their leaders.

One implication of taqiyya is that efforts to prevent Islamic attacks through mass arrests of Moslems is likely to be fruitless. The most dangerous of the attackers will be persons who appear to be anything but Moslems.

Security precautions against Assassins during the twelfth century in Cairo show us the police state Americans will live in if this war continues. After Egypt's Commander of the Armies had been killed, officials fired all government employees who were not well known to the local population. The names, addresses, "circumstances and livelihoods" of every inhabitant of the city were registered and no one was permitted to change addresses without official permission.

"There was nothing concerning the affairs of anyone in old or new Cairo that was hidden" from government officials, and anyone could be arrested at any time, wrote a chronicler.[48]

Did it work? Yes, the government's spies caught several Assassins. One was the tutor of the Caliph's children. But imagine what it was like to live in that police state.

---

[48] THE ASSASSINS, by Bernard Lewis, Oxford University Press, NY, 1967, p.61

In other words, the cost to America of siding with the Europeans against the Moslems in this Thousand Year War has already been painfully high and might soon become a lot higher. We might forfeit our Constitution.

Chris, as I said in an earlier letter, I am giving you the other side of the story, the side you are not likely to hear anywhere else. I know it is frightening, but you need to understand the past, so you can prepare for whatever the future may hold. You will not be able to predict or control what the politicians choose to do, but you can be prepared for the consequences of their actions. Let me know what you think so far.

Uncle Eric

22

High Tech and CBN

Dear Chris,

Plastic explosive is high tech stuff. It can be molded inside a telephone, coffee maker or anything else. Disguised as a cassette tape player, a small quantity blew up Pan Am flight 103 over Lockerbie, Scotland in 1988 killing 270 people.

During the Middle Ages the Assassins' favorite weapon was the dagger. Today plastic explosive is just one of the many tools a trained infiltrator might use. A sniper rifle with silencer can kill at a range of a quarter mile. Any grocery store can sell enough chemicals and poisons to kill thousands. The miniaturized, shoulder-launched guided missiles used so effectively by the Afghans against the Soviet air force could easily shoot down civilian aircraft.

The most serious threat is **CBN**.

Military weapons are of two general types, conventional and CBN. **Conventional weapons** are bullets, napalm, high-explosives and such. CBN means chemical, biological and nuclear. CBN is a whole different world, it is meant to kill thousands at a time.

CBN has long been regarded as brutal and uncivilized, and its use has been restricted. Even the Nazis, when they had their backs to the wall, did not use gas on the battlefield.

In the Iran-Iraq conflict, the U.S. and Soviet governments opened Pandora's box. The Iraqis were using nerve gas on civilians but the U.S. and Soviet governments continued helping them against Iran.

Think about it, Chris. The U.S. and Soviet governments gave their tacit approval for the use of *nerve gas* on *civilians.*

Shortly afterward, on September 9, 1988, THE WALL STREET JOURNAL quoted an unnamed U.S. official as saying "the genie is now out of the bottle."

Poison gas is called "the poor man's atomic bomb," and nerve gas is the most deadly type, one of the worst weapons known. It is colorless, odorless and silent, virtually undetectable, and if a tiny drop touches your skin you are dead within minutes. There's no good defense against it because you can't tell it's there. Invented in the 1930s, it is easy to make; it's nothing but high powered insecticide, and anyone who can make insecticide can make nerve gas.

Biological weapons are even older and easier to use. The weapons that enabled Cortez to defeat the Aztecs in 1520 were the contagious diseases spread by his soldiers; these diseases killed thousands.

> *"Experts estimate the illegal flow of weaponry and enabling technology for weapons of mass destruction from Russia alone amounts to $6 billion each year. ... There is a very real problem of the physical security of nuclear materials and facilities. ... Sophisticated terrorists could make a bomb with one to three kilograms of plutonium, and a crude bomb could be fashioned with as little as 15 kilograms of highly enriched uranium. There are about 1,200 metric tons of highly enriched uranium and 150-200 metric tons of plutonium in various facilities throughout the former Soviet Union."*
>
> *Theresa Hitchens*
> DEFENSE NEWS, *2/25/96*

And, of course, let's not forget nuclear weapons. In this age of high-tech, they have been miniaturized. A device as powerful as the Hiroshima bomb weighs less than 100 pounds and can be carried in a small suitcase or sent through the mail. One can be delivered overnight by air express to any address in the world for less than $700, with pinpoint accuracy and reliability no missile could match.

In March 1989, Israeli officials reported that the Iraqi government was engaged in a new "crash program" to develop nuclear weapons. A Navy intelligence officer told Congress that Iraq, Iran and Libya have all begun nuclear programs.

> *"The collapsing Russian economy is making Russia's estimated 650 metric tons of bomb-ready nuclear materials [it only takes a few pounds to make a bomb.—UE] more vulnerable to theft than ever. Nuclear workers have gone unpaid for months at a time. Now, with prices skyrocketing and banks refusing to disburse funds, hardships will breed desperation, creating potentially irresistible incentives to smuggle and sell these materials."*
>
> Todd Perry
> DEFENSE NEWS, *9/27/98*

In 1998, the Pakistani government, which is Moslem, demonstrated that it now has nuclear weapons.

In 1988, two Lebanese men were caught smuggling a conventional bomb across the border into Vermont. Another was caught with bombs in New Jersey.

A group called Guardians of the Islamic Revolution claimed responsibility for destroying Pan Am flight 103; the attack was believed to be retaliation for the downing of an Iranian airliner by the U.S. cruiser Vincennes.

In February 1989, California bookstores selling Salaman Rushdie's anti-Moslem book SATANIC VERSES were bombed.

Religious Nukes

Pakistan is Moslem, and India is Hindu. Ancient enemies, they are at war in the Kashmir area. This is their fourth war since 1948.

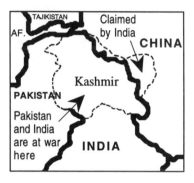

The Kashmir area is one of the most dangerous hot spots on earth. The Pakistani, Indian and Chinese regimes are all nuclear capable and none is playing with a full deck.

Pakistan is mostly Moslem, and a fierce enemy of India which is mostly Hindu.

In May 1998, India's newly elected BJP party, which is anti-Moslem, detonated five atomic bombs in the desert bordering Pakistan, breathing new life into the nuclear arms race.

The WALL STREET JOURNAL reported that, "the Clinton administration was caught flat-footed," by the explosions, and "the U.S. intelligence community was caught by surprise."

Reportedly, four of India's bombs were fission and one was thermonuclear. With sufficient uranium or plutonium, a crude fission bomb is easy to make. I talked with the inventor of the neutron bomb, Sam Cohen, who assures me a thermonuclear bomb is different, far more complex and potentially far more powerful. I think that bomb was the BJP saying, this is no cheap stunt, we're serious.

Few inhabitants of the New World have any experience with the intensity of the hatreds that are common in the Old World.

The TIMES OF INDIA newspaper says 91% of urban Indians approved of the blasts. This spectacular response certainly grabbed the attention of vote-hungry politicians all over Chaostan.

U.S. involvement in The Thousand Year War deepens. WORLD PRESS REVIEW reports that U.S. armed forces and those of the former Soviet republic of Georgia held 23 joint military exercises in 1998. Georgia is 83% Eastern Orthodox Christian and has been fighting an intermittent war with the Moslem Abkhaz.

After demonstrating their bombs, Indian politicians said, now that we have the bomb we plan to take Kashmir. The two sides, India and Pakistan, began shelling each other in Kashmir.

Chris, in east Europe and Asia, religion is politics. Chaostan has a Hindu bomb (India's), an Islamic bomb (Pakistan's), an Eastern Orthodox Christian bomb (Russia's) and a Jewish bomb (Israel's).

Old antagonists, all these cultures are becoming more militantly religious, and each believes it has God on its side. An interesting situation, where do you suppose it is leading?[49]

In 1993 the World Trade Center was bombed by an Islamic group.

I fear most for the Israelis. When U.S. officials continued helping the Iraqi government despite Iraqi use of nerve gas on civilians, they were automatically writing off the Israelis. Israel is within easy range of missile and artillery nerve gas weapons. Trade minister Ariel Sharon said, "I don't think I've ever been worried as I am worried now. ... They used gas. Nobody said a word about it. The world kept quiet."[50]

Each time one of the gangster governments in the Mideast is overthrown, that government's weapons fall into the hands of the rebels. Some of the rebels are civilized, but others are

---

[49] Read Mark Twain's "The War Prayer."

[50] WALL STREET JOURNAL, February 22, 1989, p.A17. Actually Sharon is not completely accurate. U.S. officials did complain but they continued helping the Iraqis.

products of a thousand years of European brutality, they're as rabid as the gangsters they replace.

When the Libyan government was overthrown in 1969 the weapons fell into the hands of Qadaffi. When the Shah of Iran was overthrown in 1979 his weapons ended up with Khomeini. When Syria's Salah Jadid was overthrown, his weapons ended up with Hafez Assad, and when Iraq's Ahmad Hassan al-Bakr was overthrown, his weapons became the property of Saddam Hussein.

Many Islamic governments distribute weapons freely to enemies of the West. Pakistani rulers helped the Afghans against the Russians. Qadaffi is known to have helped the IRA against the British.

In May 1987, U.S. NEWS & WORLD REPORT revealed that Khomeini had offered to help Nicaraguan rulers form joint "Iranian-Latin terror teams inside the U.S." Did they do it? If so, where are these teams now?

Remember, Chris, the Islamic world has a different time perspective than we do. They have a long history of planning ten or twenty years ahead for an attack.

The CBN monster has been released from his cage. We don't know who has these weapons or where they will use them. We know only that by backing the Iraqi government in its war against Iran, the U.S. and Russian governments approved the precedent for the use of these weapons.

Okay, you say, I make a strong case for America to declare neutrality and withdraw from the Thousand Year War. But what about the oil and other natural resources in the Islamic world? Don't we need these raw materials?

Yes, we need the Moslems' raw materials.

And, they need our money.

If the Iraqis or Iranians get the Persian Gulf oil fields, what will they do with the oil? Drink it?

No, they will need to sell it.

Yes, they might try to sell it at a higher price than we want to pay. Should we fight a war to lower the price?

How much blood are you willing to pay for a barrel of oil? And, are you willing to pay with your own blood, or only with that of young soldiers who understand nothing about the Thousand Year War?

Chris, if I am sounding harsh, I apologize. Few subjects are as serious as the Thousand Year War. My goal is not to be cheerful, or objective, but to give you the other side of the story, the non-statist side you are not likely to get anywhere else.

Uncle Eric

23

Loyalty of Russian Troops

Dear Chris,

For decades Americans were taught that the Soviet bloc was a huge monolithic empire. Nothing could have been further from the truth. The Soviet bloc consisted of more than 250 nationalities and cultures that shared no language or traditions.

The only thing these groups had in common was that they had been **subjugated** by the ruthless Moscow regime, and most of them hated this regime.

Hundreds of thousands of the troops in the Soviet armed forces were Moslems. When these troops were sent into Afghanistan they refused to fight. Their loyalty to their Moslem cousins was stronger than their loyalty to Moscow. They were pulled out and replaced by non-Moslem troops from northern regions.

With so much of its army disloyal, the Soviet empire finally fell apart. By 1992 it had become 15 separate nations.

Chris, the 50 million Moslems in these nations are still there, and they still hate Moscow. We have no way of knowing what kind of secret plans they might be making.

Uncle Eric

24

Loyalty of American Troops

Dear Chris,

After the unrestricted submarine warfare and bombings of cities during the two world wars, U.S. military personnel went through a period of soul-searching over the morality of their jobs. After the bombings of Hiroshima and Nagasaki, Chief of Staff Admiral Leahy said these bombings were not necessary, Japan had been bottled up by the naval blockade and was no longer a threat, and he worried that, "we had adopted an ethical standard common to the barbarians of the Dark Age."[51]

During the 1950s and '60s, the soul-searching intensified as soldiers, sailors and airmen wondered if they would really drop atomic bombs on millions of men, women and children if they were ordered to do it.

Vietnam raised this soul-searching to fever pitch. Military officers knew their willingness to go anywhere and do anything they had been told had led to their own misuse and abuse.

Younger troops in today's forces may believe in blind obedience but the older officers no longer do. They know their oath requires them to support and defend the Constitu-

---

[51] HISTORY OF THE SECOND WORLD WAR by B.H. Liddell Hart, Perigee Books, 1971, p.695

tion of the United States against all enemies foreign and domestic but it says nothing about blind obedience. Let me emphasize that the oath says *all* enemies, including domestic ones, even if these domestic ones are the politicians giving the orders.

Today's officers take this oath seriously. They are true professionals fiercely dedicated to defending their homeland and the Constitution but quick to doubt orders that are not clearly related to defense.

This became captivatingly apparent during a nationally broadcast 1987 television panel discussion about military ethics. A Marine colonel was asked the theoretical question, "What would you do if you were ordered to take no prisoners?" ("Take no prisoners" is military code meaning all the enemy should be killed, their surrender will not be accepted.) Without hesitation the colonel looked squarely at the questioner and, right in front of the TV cameras, stated he would disobey. It was dramatic.

The colonel explained, "Presumably we have gone to war to fight an evil — that's the only reason we went to war — and if you obey that order you've just become the thing you are fighting. I won't do it." [52]

This is deep thinking. It is individualism in the finest American tradition and it is far from the old military ethic of blind obedience. It adds more uncertainty to the course of the Thousand Year War.

Chris, how will U.S. troops and officers react as they learn more about this conflict? What will they do when they realize they have been ordered to risk their lives in a medieval religious war that has been raging for a thousand years?

Uncle Eric

---

[52] PBS series "Ethics In America," recorded October 31, 1987

25

Why Die For An Interest?

Dear Chris,

U.S. officials have never understood the Thousand Year War. Why, I don't know, maybe they don't want to.

Sirhan Sirhan was a supporter of Robert F. Kennedy during Kennedy's 1968 presidential campaign. Kennedy had voiced support for the downtrodden, which was music to Sirhan's ears. Sirhan was concerned about the Palestinians.

Then on May 26th of that year Kennedy made a speech in which he advocated sending fifty F-4 Phantom jets to Israel. Ten days later Sirhan killed him.

As if Kennedy's death were some kind of accident unrelated to the war, U.S. officials steadily broadened their involvement in it, and have continued to do so for more than thirty years.

When U.S. Marines were sent into Lebanon in 1983 they were told they would be neutral peacekeepers. They were ordered to keep a low profile and remain lightly armed so as not to intimidate the persons they were sent to protect. They were policemen.

But after the Marines were in, President Reagan abandoned neutrality and sided with the Christians. When Marine

commander Colonel Geraghty learned that naval bombard-
ment would be used not to protect his Marines but to help the
Christians, he got on his radio and argued vehemently, "This
will cost us our neutrality. Do you realize if you do that, we'll
get slaughtered down here? We could be severely attacked.
We're totally vulnerable. We're sitting ducks."[53]

Geraghty's warnings were ignored and 241 Marines were
killed when Moslems retaliated using a truck bomb. In
Washington the deaths were chalked up to "terrorism," and
U.S. involvement in the Thousand Year War continued.

In 1996, 19 more Americans were killed in a truck bomb
attack in Saudi Arabia, a nearly identical copy of the attack
13 years earlier.

In 1998, two U.S. embassies were bombed in Africa,
another nearly identical repeat of the 1983 attack.

More such incidents are surely coming, yet Americans
never question their government's involvement in the Thousand Year War. The attacks are always blamed on "terrorism," as if this were the full and complete explanation. No
one ever asks, why do those people hate us so much?

The confusion about why we are in the war can be seen in
the use of the word "interests." At one time, American troops
were expected to risk their lives fighting for liberty. Later the
cause worth dying for was downgraded to democracy. Now
it is interests.

Chris, I have been watching the use of the word interests
grow for twenty years, and in the 1990s, interests became the
mantra of U.S. foreign policy. In the February 3, 1997, ARMY
TIMES,[54] for instance, reporter Rick Maze described Defense

---

[53] SACRED RAGE by Robin Wright, Simon & Schuster, 1986, p.78
[54] Page 13

Secretary Cohen's statements to the Armed Services Committee. Said Cohen, "Military forces should only be used if they advance U.S. interests."

What's an interest?

On November 15, 1996, President Clinton said that U.S. troops would stay in Bosnia and wherever else "our interests are clear."[55]

What's an interest?

In Hillary Clinton's Internet column on April 4, 1996, she said, "Our military power is enhancing our interests."

Again, what's an interest?

In the July 25, 1994 issue of U.S. NEWS & WORLD REPORT, you will find the complaint by former U.S. ambassador Roger Harrison that "Every half-baked general and warlord in the world feels free to ignore our interests."[56]

In the November 13, 1998 WALL STREET JOURNAL[57] we find a similar complaint from former assistant undersecretary of defense for policy planning Zalmay Khalilzad. Mr. Khalilzad argues for military action against Iraq because the Iraqi government is a "significant obstacle to U.S. regional interests."

And — a final example — on December 16, 1998, explaining why he bombed Iraqis, killing an estimated 2000 people the day before his impeachment was to be voted on, President Clinton said it was "to protect the national interest of the United States."

I have searched the Constitution for a definition of the word interests, but found none, and I don't know anyone who

---

[55] "U.S. Pullout From Bosnia Is Delayed," SACRAMENTO BEE, November 16, 1996, p.1
[56] Page 22
[57] Page 18

knows what the word means. All we know for sure about an interest is that U.S. soldiers, sailors and airmen are expected to fight and die for it.

Chris, after spending four years in the Air Force during the Vietnam War, I came to the conclusion that, knowing what I know now, the only thing I would be willing to die for is my home and family; I would do whatever it takes to repel an invader, to protect my homeland. When I am deciding what I think of a U.S. military operation in some far off corner of the world, I always ask the question, would this be worth *my* life? If the answer is no, then I don't think it would be worth anyone else's life either. One thing I can tell you with great certainty is that I would not be willing to die for an interest.

Keep an eye out for the word interests, I think you will see a lot of it in months and years to come, but I bet you won't find an explanation of what it is or why it is worth a soldier's life.

As I said, we are in the Thousand Year War but no one knows why.

Uncle Eric

26

Some Economics
of the Thousand Year War

Dear Chris,

Let me draw a few ideas from previous letters to give you the Thousand Year War in a nutshell:

Iran is Persia. The Persian Gulf is called the Persian Gulf because for more than two thousand years it belonged to Persia, until the governments of Britain and the U.S. came into the area and took control.

In the 1990s, Washington kept about two dozen warships in the Persian Gulf.

How many Persian warships have you seen in Chesapeake Bay?

In short, they aren't over here, we are over there. They are on the defense, we are on the offense.

Who do you think has been violating the fundamental law, do not encroach on other persons or their property?

Further, there is a very serious angle to this defense vs. offense situation, because the relationship between defensive and offensive weapons has changed in recent years.

Back in World War II, the costs of defensive and offensive weapons were roughly equal.

For instance, the batteries of antiaircraft guns and squadrons of pursuit aircraft were roughly equal in cost to the squadrons of bombers they were trying to shoot down. The ratio of defensive to offensive costs was roughly 1 to 1.

Now we are in the age of inexpensive high-tech, and the high-tech advancements have affected defensive weapons more than offensive weapons. The missile that kills a tank costs only $5,000, the tank costs a million or more.

The missile that kills a jet fighter costs $50,000, the fighter costs $100 million.

The new electronic decoys of tanks and radar equipment are extremely effective and cost only $3,000 each; the missiles wasted on them can cost a million dollars each.

In the Thousand Year War the U.S. and its European allies are on the bad side of that equation. The Islamic enemy's military forces are not over here, ours are over there; we are on the offense.

Look at what happened in the Iraq-Kuwait war. Iraq was a little tin-pot dictatorship with an economy the size of South Carolina's. Yet the U.S. had to use fully half its non-nuclear military force — the most powerful military force ever seen on earth. In a single month U.S. officials spent tens of billions of dollars, and the best they were able to achieve with this expenditure was a stalemate. Far from an unconditional surrender, the Iraqi Baathist regime is still in power clearly planning who knows what kind of new trouble for the West.

This change in the defensive vs. offensive ratio is striking. The top fighter aircraft of World War II was the P-51; the top fighter today is the F-15. Offensive weapons are so expensive today that if we adjust all the numbers for **inflation** we find that when one F-15 is shot down, this is equivalent to losing eight and a half *squadrons* of P-51's. (Figuring ten planes per squadron.)

Chris, this may be the most important reason the Russians lost in Afghanistan. Using the P-51 as our economic "unit of account," an Afghan guerrilla with a Stinger missile was using one-seventh of a P-51 to shoot down 85 P-51's.

Who can afford that? That's a defensive vs. offensive cost ratio of 1 to 600. In World War II it was 1 to 1, now 1 to 600. On the basis of this example, to be on equal footing today, the offense must spend six *hundred* times as much as the defense.

That's one reason the economic effects of the Thousand Year War are likely to be devastating if the U.S. stays in it.

No one really knows the true costs of the Iraq-Kuwait war, the estimates run from $400 million per day to $4 billion per day.

Those are big numbers, let's try to get a handle on how big they really are. We'll take the middle range of $2 billion per day.

Imagine walking into a new car dealership, a Volvo dealership, to look at the new Volvos. Imagine taking a test drive. Nice car. Leather seats. Stereo. Air conditioning.

Now imagine pushing this new Volvo over a cliff and seeing it burst into flames as it smashes on the rocks below.

Then imagine pushing 100,000 new Volvos over a cliff. Every day.

Now you have an idea of the economic cost of this war.

In Vietnam the cost of killing one enemy soldier was $16,000. In Iraq, $500,000.

In August 1998 President Clinton ordered the U.S. armed forces to fire approximately 75 cruise missiles at targets in Afghanistan and Sudan. Each missile cost one million dollars.

Chris, if we do not get out of this war, I think the taxes and inflation will be horrible. Then add the fact that the supplies of raw materials — the iron, oil, tin, copper, lumber, gold, silver and so forth — from that part of the world will be disrupted, and you can see this war could turn out to be an astounding economic disaster as well as a great waste of lives.

Uncle Eric

27

Go to High Risk Areas?

Dear Chris,

America entered the Thousand Year War two centuries ago in the Barbary Wars. One of the worst parts of this conflict was the precedent it set for U.S. military protection of Americans abroad.

In the Barbary Wars, U.S. merchantmen were sailing through high risk areas. When they got into trouble the owners of the ships used their political influence to have the Navy sent to rescue them.

American sailors and marines died for the merchant crews who should never have been in those areas in the first place.

The precedent haunts us today. As far as I know, Americans are the only people on earth who still assume they can go anywhere they want and if they get into trouble the marines will be sent to rescue them. In most cases this assumption is wrong, the marines will not be sent, but many Americans behave as if they will. They travel into high risk areas, they invest in high risk areas, they set up businesses in high risk areas, and then when the shooting starts, they scream for the government to send help.

So, U.S. officials intervene in every corner of the globe and get into one war after another.

The only way to put a stop to this insanity is for U.S. officials to announce that the blanket world-wide protection is ended. Inside your homeland you can expect all the protection the armed forces can muster, but when you go abroad, you go at your own risk. If you don't like the risk, don't go.

These are the same terms under which citizens of the other 200 or so countries on earth do their foreign business and traveling, and I believe Americans should live under these terms, too.

After all, if a citizen of Brazil, Australia or Nigeria gets mugged in Peoria, do you think he expects his country's army to come to his rescue?

If a German or Japanese business in California or New York finds itself in trouble with the governments of these states, how would Americans feel about German or Japanese paratroopers landing in California or New York?

Citizens of every other country know that when they go abroad they go at their own risk. If they don't like the risk, they don't go.

Unfortunately, I don't expect this reasoning to be adopted in Washington, at least not during my lifetime, so the precedent set in the Barbary Wars will stand. Americans will continue traveling and doing business in high risk areas, thereby providing lots of excuses for power junkies to get deeper into the Thousand Year War.

Chris, the war blows hot and cold. Sometimes Mideast conflicts are in the news daily and other times we hear nothing for months. It's been this way for a thousand years and I see no reason to expect a change until the lid finally blows off and we are in another fully developed world war.

When will this be? I wish I knew. Maybe in twenty years, maybe in twenty minutes.

What will our daily lives be like when it does happen? Previous incidents give us some hints. Three examples:

1. During the Iran-Iraq conflict in the 1980s, more than 500 commercial ships were damaged or sunk. Warships of seven navies were used to keep the oil flowing. Without these navy ships, the price of oil would have been much higher, and we could have seen the high consumer prices and unemployment we saw during the oil crises of the 1970s. Today, with the Cold War ended, the U.S. and other major powers have cut back their navies to the point that there may not be enough warships to keep the oil lanes open in the event of another big Persian Gulf war.

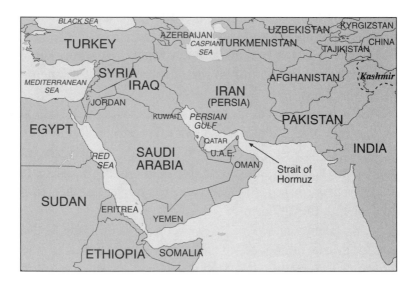

The Persian Gulf has 65% of the total world oil supply. Most of the oil is held by the U.S.-backed dictatorships on the west side. Iraq and Iran plan to take it.

2. When President Carter froze Iranian (Persian) assets during the 1979 embassy hostage crisis, wealthy Arabs became fearful that their assets would be **frozen**, too. They bailed out of dollar assets, and this triggered a world-wide run on the dollar. Interest rates shot up three points in one month. The panic out of dollars became a panic into precious metals, and gold ran up to $850 and silver to $50. There is nothing to keep it from happening again.[58]

3. After the 1973 Arab-Israeli war, Arab governments retaliated against U.S. support for Israel by raising oil prices. Price hikes continued throughout the 1970's until hundreds of billions of dollars of American wealth had been siphoned off to the Mideast. It's a safe bet that Islamic governments would love to do the same thing to us again, and if Iran, Iraq, Saudi Arabia, Kuwait and the other oil producers of the Persian Gulf will kiss and make up with each other, I am sure they will give it another try.

That's just three of the many ways the Thousand Year War could affect us.

Chris, in one of my earlier letters I said events on the other side of the world a thousand years ago affect us more than events in our hometowns today. I think you can see now that I was not exaggerating.

When this war does finally become fully developed, how bad will it be?

---

[58] This is fully explained in THE MONEY MYSTERY by Richard Maybury, Bluestocking Press, Placerville, CA, 95667.

Again we cannot know. Unless it goes nuclear, I don't think it will be as bad as World War II. I'm expecting something on the scale of World War I but that's only a guess. The point I am most confident about is that when it finally happens the world economy and investment markets will be shaken.

Watch Saudi Arabia, it's the big prize. Saudi dictators control oceans of oil plus Islam's two holiest cities, Mecca and Medina. They claim to be anti-Russian, so President Reagan promised U.S. military support to protect them against all threats including internal uprisings by their own people.[59]

I wonder how many U.S. troops know they have been committed to protect the Saudi dictators against these dictators' own people.

Let me emphasize, Chris, that in my opinion there is nothing Americans or their government can do to end the Thousand Year War. The hatreds are too old, complex and intense, and too far outside our experience. If you find this hard to believe, read Robert Kaplan's fine book BALKAN GHOSTS about the hatreds in the Balkans.

There was a day when Americans could have been neutral mediators between the Islamic world and the West, and between regimes in the Islamic world. But this neutrality was seriously damaged in the Barbary Wars, and since World War II it has been entirely demolished by our government's alliances and interventions.

As far as I can see, the only realistic course for America now would be for our government to sever all political

---

[59] Gerald F. Sieb, "Reagan Asserts U.S. Will Defend Saudi Arabia," WALL STREET JOURNAL, October 2, 1981, p.1

connections with all parties involved in the war, apologize to everyone and admit we didn't know what we were getting into. Then *leave the Islamic world alone!*

After a century or so, U.S. officials might send a polite letter asking if anyone over there wants to be friends, but I am sure any overture sooner than that would be too soon, those people have long memories.

During that century-long cooling-off period, private individuals and firms could visit and do business with people in the Islamic world, but in no way should they ever claim they represent anyone except themselves. This way, the risk is limited, if they make a mistake, they will be the only ones likely to pay for it.

Again, Chris, please read BALKAN GHOSTS, and remember that the hatreds you are tasting in that book are typical of all of Chaostan.

Uncle Eric

28

A Small But Revealing
Research Project

Dear Chris,

In the spirit of continuing to give you the other side of the story — the non-statist side you are not likely to get anywhere else — here is a suggestion for a research project.

Around the world, Americans are generally regarded as some of the most kind and charitable people on earth. Whenever there is an earthquake or other disaster, or widespread poverty or disease, the first help to arrive is often from America. Foreigners are amazed and impressed at this generosity. America's private charities do wonderful work.

But, the U.S. government is something entirely different than the American people or the private charities they support. The government does send a lot of aid overseas, but much of this aid goes to other governments, not to the people who live under these governments.

Chris, ask a librarian to steer you in the direction of the answers to two questions:

1. Which governments get money or other kinds of assistance from Washington, and how much do they get?

2. What is this money really used for?

On this second question, *do not settle for the propaganda about the use of the money, examine the actual behavior of the recipient governments.*

It is very important to keep in mind that money is fungible. This means one dollar can substitute for any other dollar. When, say, the Egyptian government gets two billion dollars from Washington, this is two billion of its own money it does not need to spend on whatever it might have. Two billion of U.S. money spent on bread for the poor is two billion that Egyptian officials do not need to spend on bread, so it is two billion they can spend on bullets to keep the poor from overthrowing their tyrannical government.

A good way to go at the research is to approach it backwards. First search news magazines for information about what foreign governments are doing to their own people. Then go to the STATISTICAL ABSTRACT OF THE U.S. and other official records to find out how much help each of these governments gets from Washington. Again, keep in mind that money is fungible, a dollar these governments do not need to spend on bread, medicine or blankets is a dollar they can use to buy bullets.

So, what is your tax money being used for abroad, really? Here are a few examples to get you started.

Washington backs the Russian government — gives it money and helps train its troops — and the Russian government has killed tens of thousands of Chechens.

In Iran, Washington backed the Shah and his secret police for 25 years, and then backed Saddam Hussein when Saddam Hussein attacked Iran in 1980. Washington has helped kidnap, torture and kill hundreds of thousands of Iranians.

Lebanon. Do you remember studying about the battleship New Jersey shelling Moslem villages in 1983? Washington took sides with the Christians against the Moslems.

During the war in Bosnia in the 1990s, Washington and NATO levied an arms embargo on Bosnia. Gun controls. The Serbs were already heavily armed, so the embargo left the Moslems with no way to defend themselves, and tens of thousands were killed.

Washington now has troops in 144 countries[60] — that's about 2/3 of all the countries in the world — and in most cases, these American troops are there to support the regimes that control these countries.

All these regimes have enemies, so now their enemies are our enemies.

Few Americans realize that in the conquest of the Philippines a century ago, the U.S. Army was used to kill 220,000 Filipino men, women and children.[61] It was ethnic cleansing just like in Bosnia today.

In the 1990s, during the Turk's war against the Kurds, Turks were killing the Kurds, the Greeks were helping the Kurds,[62] and Washington backed both the Turks and the Greeks. In short, Washington was indirectly helping to both protect and kill the Kurds.

---

[60] Air Force Times, August 3, 1998, p.31

[61] Wall Street Journal, "The Death Toll of the Bells of Balangiga," November 19, 1997, p. A6,

[62] Economist, August 1, 1998, p.45

U.S. tax dollars at work.

During the 1990s, the Indonesian army killed some 200,000 people on the island of East Timor,[63] and Washington backed the Indonesian army, provided them with weapons and training.

You might also look into the career of Manuel Noriega and his connections with the CIA, and what happened to Cuban rebels at the Bay of Pigs.

Chris, the American government is not the American people, and the American people know very little about what their government does in other countries. The other side of the story is not pretty but it is revealing. It explains why so many foreigners have such mixed feelings about America, sometimes hating us and sometimes loving us.

Uncle Eric

---

[63] "US Aids Killers In Indonesia," article in The Nation magazine, reprinted in the Sacramento Bee, 29 Mar 98.

29

Liberty Not Democracy

Dear Chris,

The wars spreading across Chaostan have many causes but one of the most important is that democracy is not liberty. Liberty is protection of the individual's rights to his life, freedom and property. Democracy is majority rule, and majority rule is mob rule.

The U.S. government and the United Nations are tireless in promoting democracy, and have convinced much of the world to strive for it. In Sri Lanka, an island country off the coast of India, we see a microcosm of their handiwork, and an example of where the whole world is headed.

Sri Lanka has two nationalities, the Sinhalese and the Tamil. The Sinhalese are the majority. Being democratic, they have enacted laws allowing them to sponge off the Tamils.

The Tamils want to split and form their own country, and the Sinhalese, who do not want to lose their milk cow, won't let them. Result: war.

The U.S. government and the United Nations have little interest in liberty. Liberty would drastically reduce their power. They want democracy, majority rule. So, it does not take a rocket scientist to see where this is leading.

The world contains some 10,000 nationalities[64] living under about 220 governments.

Four of the most dangerous wars (the Balkans, Chechnya, Azerbaijan and Tajikistan) are all due to minority nationalities being afraid to live under the rule of the majorities that dominate them.

Chris, it is impossible to know exactly how things will unfold except to say that chaos will spread until countries embrace liberty, and that day is, I'm afraid, a long way off.

Uncle Eric

---

[64] As defined by language and custom.

30

Summary

Dear Chris,

Before I end this series of letters I will give you my usual summary.

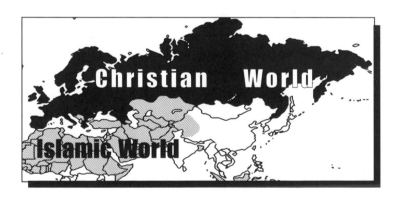

1.   These letters have made no attempt to be objective. My goal was to give you the other side of the story, the non-statist side you are not likely to get anywhere else. The non-statist view was explained in my previous sets of

letters.[65] This view is based on the two fundamental laws taught by all religions: (1) do all you have agreed to do and (2) do not encroach on other persons or their property.

2. Few Americans have any idea what their government has done in foreign countries.

3. We are in a war between Europe and the Islamic world. European rulers started the war a thousand years ago, in the Crusades, and the U.S. got into it during the Barbary Wars two centuries ago on "the shores of Tripoli."

4. In the Mideast, religion and politics are the same thing. This is a religious war.

5. In its present form, this Thousand Year War is the Islamic world against, primarily, the U.S., Russia and Israel, and secondarily against the Europeans. As the Europeans have tried to back away, the U.S. has stepped in to take their place.

6. Moslems have *nine centuries* of experience at covert warfare. We have no way of knowing what they are capable of, and to believe their "terrorism" can be stopped is to believe in magic.

7. All Islamic governments are ruthless dictatorships that represent no one but themselves. They are the enemies

---

[65] Especially in the book WHATEVER HAPPENED TO JUSTICE? by Richard Maybury, Bluestocking Press, Placerville, CA, 95667.

of their people and their people hate them. Nearly all these governments were established by the Europeans as puppets, or they are rebel regimes that came to power after overthrowing the European puppets. Not one of these governments has any interest in genuine liberty. When U.S. officials claim a Mideast country is on their side, they are talking only about the dozens or hundreds of people at the top of the government, not the millions in the general population.

8. In 1948, with the creation of the Jewish state of Israel, European Jews leaped into the middle of this Thousand Year War. Few of them had even the foggiest understanding of what they were getting into.

9. Moslems have suffered at the hands of European governments every bit as much as Jews.

10. Washington maintains its closest alliances with the European governments.

11. One of the world's oldest and most intense hatreds is that between Russians and Turks. Russia's heritage is Eastern Orthodox Christian, and Turkey's is Moslem. Other Eastern Orthodox Christians traditionally sympathetic to the Russians against the Turks are the Serbs, Georgians, Armenians, Ukrainians, Romanians and Greeks.

12. The hatred between Sunni Moslems and Shiite Moslems is at least as old and intense as that between Moslems and Europeans.

13. The American military's Achilles heel is guerrilla war.

14. Americans have been taught to be Europhiles. They do not realize they owe as much to the Islamic world as they do to Europe. During Europe's Dark Ages, the Moslems and Jews in the Islamic world rescued and advanced the science, math and technology that made our world possible.

15. The West sees each outbreak of violence as a new war. The Islamic world has a different view of time and sees each outbreak as another chapter in the same war.

16. There is little Americans or their government can do to broker an end to this war, at least not in our lifetimes, because the American government has thrown away its neutrality.

17. No one knows exactly why America is in this war other than to say it is for our "interests."

18. Islamic groups and governments occasionally form alliances with western governments, to play westerners against each other.

19. Many groups and governments in the Mideast hate each other but they hate us more, so they occasionally form temporary alliances against us.

20. Most Moslems are fine people but millions have been pushed to the breaking point.

21. Most "terrorists" are independent, they have no allegiance to any nation. In most cases, their allegiance is to their religion.

22. Until the 1980's the weapons used in this war were conventional, but now they are moving into the realm of CBN (chemical, biological, nuclear). No one in the world has a good defense against covertly delivered CBN weapons.

23. If you remember nothing else from these letters, remember this: *Not since the Middle Ages have Moslem armies threatened an invasion of Europe, but since that time there has hardly been any five-year period in which European troops have not been under arms on Moslem soil.*[66]

24. At least 75% of the world's oil is under the homelands of Moslems.

25. Their armies are not over here, ours are over there.

Chris, I have been writing articles about the Thousand Year War for almost twenty years. After an article is published I usually hear from angry people who denounce me for opposing the Crusades. "The Moslems started it!" they will scream. "Moslems took Jerusalem in 638! The Europeans had every right to take it back! Islam is evil, we must continue this fight with every weapon we have!"

---

[66] Godfrey Jansen quoted in SACRED RAGE by Robin Wright, Simon & Schuster, 1986, p.252

I have run into this response often, but each time it still shocks me that an American could be so thoroughly brainwashed by the European view of history. These people have a blind loyalty to Europe, as if European rulers never did anything wrong.

These enraged responses have convinced me that the hatred from this war runs so deep that there is no hope of ending it in our lifetimes or even in the lifetimes of our grandchildren

I believe the only rational way for America to deal with the Thousand Year War is for our government to withdraw from the Islamic world. Americans should be friends with everyone over there, conduct trade with them and visit them, but *no political connections* with anyone.

And, admit we did not understand what we were getting into. Apologize for siding with the Europeans and get out now.

Uncle Eric

31

The Murderous Cycle

Dear Chris,

Each time an incident happens, try to see the war from the other side's point of view. If you were them, what would you be doing to get western governments out of your homeland?

Israel and America have been plunged into the midst of a thousand year cycle of murder and reprisal that few Israelis or Americans understand. None of it is justifiable and our allies, the Europeans and the surrogate regimes they established in the Islamic world, are as guilty as our enemies. This is not a movie, there are no good guys or bad guys, just the wounded and the dead.

> "I have ever deemed it fundamental for the United States never to take active part in the quarrels of Europe. Their political interests are entirely distinct from ours. Their mutual jealousies, their balance of power, their complicated alliances, their forms and principles of government, are all foreign to us. They are nations of eternal war."
>
> — Thomas Jefferson, 1823

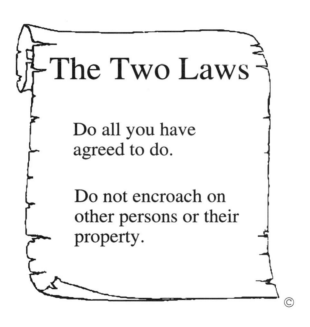

The Two Laws

Do all you have
agreed to do.

Do not encroach on
other persons or their
property.

©

The two laws that make civilization possible.

Spread the Word!

Jefferson was President during the Barbary Wars. He was a brilliant man, too bad he ignored his own advice. I suppose this is just one more example of the fact that political power corrupts one's judgment.

The Thousand Year War is a result of the fact that Europe's rulers, and now America's, have consistently violated the fundamental law that forbids encroachment. Islamic armies are not over here, ours are over there.

The bloodshed cannot end until the two laws are obeyed. Spread the word.

Uncle Eric

American University

In the 1800s, Christian missionaries traveled from New England to the Islamic world to make converts. They quickly learned that Europeans had been there before them, and the Europeans had left the Moslems in no frame of mind to consider adopting Christianity.

The missionaries decided to try to persuade the Moslems that America was different. Unlike Europe, America and its religions were dedicated to liberty, including religious liberty.

To open the Islamic world's mind to the American way, the Christian missionaries established American University in Beirut, Lebanon in 1866.

When the cornerstone of a new building at the university was laid in 1871, Daniel Bliss, the college's first president said,

> "This college is for all conditions and classes of men without regard to color, nationality, race or religion. A man white, black or yellow, Christian, Jew, Mohammedan or heathen, may enter and enjoy all the advantages of this institution."[67]

This small patch of America so distant from its New England roots became a magnet for intellectuals from all over the Islamic world.

[67] THE ARABISTS by Robert D. Kaplan, The Free Press, NY 1933, p.36

Schooled in modern science and math as well as America's political philosophy, these intellectuals graduated from American University, fanned out across the Moslem world and began to influence their people and their governments. American University became the most important and beneficial western institution in the Mideast.

Then, after World War II, the U.S. government became deeply involved in the Islamic world, and the wonderful progress American University had made in building friendship between America and the Islamic world was swept away.

You can read about American University and the Christian missionaries' attempts to get us out of the Thousand Year War in the fascinating 1993 book THE ARABISTS by Robert Kaplan.

32

The New Wars In Chaostan

Dear Chris,

The evidence is strong that the inhabitants of East Europe, Asia and North Africa are returning to their old ways, meaning war. This is a very conservative forecast that should raise no eyebrows. For thousands of years war has been the normal condition of that area, which I call Chaostan. I would be predicting something new and unbelievable only if I were predicting peace.

I do not believe these wars will be as bad as World War II. They will probably be something on the scale of World War I, admittedly perhaps with some limited use of nuclear, chemical and biological weapons. I repeat, limited, and not necessarily dangerous to America.

We could see a replay of the 1800s. Europe and Asia were wracked by war, and flight capital (money) poured into America. This deluge of money lined the pockets of investors, business people and workers who took advantage of it.

That's how things should work again. How they will work may be, unfortunately, a different matter. If the U.S. government continues meddling in these wars then I am not so optimistic.

For most of the 1800s the U.S. government stayed out of other people's wars. In the 1900s powerseekers changed the meaning of the word neutrality. It now means isolationism.

How deeply is war ingrained in the psyches of Moslems and European Christians? During the Middle Ages, Europeans removed huge stone obelisks from Egypt. You can see them all over Rome. They still stand in the city squares, still topped by crosses and other Christian symbols to indicate that Christianity will conquer Islam.

Today's wars in the Balkans, Chechnya, Azerbaijan and Tajikistan are the resurgence of these ancient hatreds.

On April 28, 1995, the French government banned a new Islamic book saying it is anti-Western and contrary to French national values.

Turkey is Moslem and its largest city is Istanbul. Turks captured Istanbul in 1453 but today, five centuries later, Christians in the eastern Mediterranean still call the city by it's old Christian name, Constantinople.

No, Chris, the sky is not falling, but I am afraid another chapter in the Thousand Year War between the Islamic world and the West is now being written.

Uncle Eric

Appendix

A Brief History
of the Iraq-Kuwait War

Extracted from
Richard Maybury's Early Warning Report Newsletter

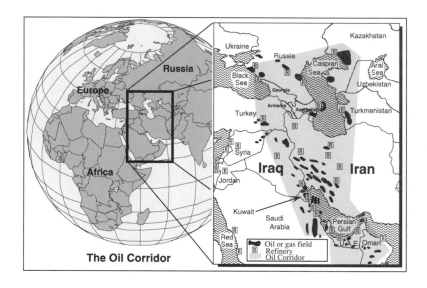

The Oil Corridor

At least 70% of the total world oil supply is in the oil corridor. The two most dangerous enemies of the West — Iraq and Iran — are in the exact center of it.

In the Islamic world anyone who stands up to the West and survives is a hero. Saddam Hussein not only survived the 1990-91 Iraq-Kuwait war, he outlasted his opponents. President Bush, Prime Minister Thatcher and President Gorbachev are all out of power now, but Saddam remains. In his culture this makes him the winner of that 43-day war.

It's like this. Suppose a high school football team challenges the Los Angeles Rams. The game starts and the Rams instantly score a touchdown. Then the high schoolers run one play and fumble. But after a peek at the high schoolers' *strategy* the Rams get scared and go home, leaving the high schoolers alone on the field with 59 minutes left to play.

Who won the game?

What was the Iraqi strategy that so frightened President Bush? We cannot know what Mr. Bush or Saddam Hussein were thinking, but here is my guess.

Saddam is known to be an avid student of the Vietnam war. He surely understands that the U.S. military's Achilles heel is guerrilla war. The only way to win a guerrilla war is to go into any village suspected of supporting the guerrillas and kill every man, woman and child, and Americans won't do this. They hate to murder women and children, so they are very poor at fighting guerrillas.

I think Saddam Hussein burned the oil fields and committed other atrocities to lure President Bush into sending U.S. forces into central Iraq after him, to generate a house-to-house guerrilla war.

Saddam's strategy was to sacrifice his least effective troops. He wanted the U.S. to kill tens of thousands, thereby creating horror throughout the Islamic world and triggering the overthrow of all the Moslem rulers who were allied with Bush. It was beginning to work. Moslems from Morocco to Indonesia were becoming enraged at the slaughter. In a few months the whole Moslem world would have swung behind Saddam.

In short, Saddam used himself as bait to lure the U.S. into a guerrilla war with the whole Islamic world that would have gone on for decades. When Mr. Bush realized what he had blundered into, he withdrew and left the football field after only one minute of play. General Schwartzkopf admitted this when he said U.S. forces were not sent into central Iraq after Saddam because it would have become "a tarpit."

U.S. officials paint Saddam as a fool. This is dangerous. Saddam might be insane but he is not stupid. He is as brilliant as he is evil.

Note that most of the troops slaughtered by the U.S. were not Sunnis, they were Shiites, the people who wanted to overthrow Saddam. The Iraqi leader had suckered U.S. officials into killing their most important Iraqi *allies*.

The Iraqi cleverness continues. Deploying U.S. forces to the Persian Gulf is monstrously expensive. Saddam now knows that without firing a shot he can run up the U.S. budget deficit at will, simply by harassing the UN weapons inspectors and causing U.S. officials to deploy ships, planes and troops to the Persian Gulf.

The deployments also put great strain on the marriages and families of U.S. military personnel, causing many to leave the service, depleting America's reservoir of military skills and experience. DEFENSE NEWS reports that during the 1990s, so many Air Force pilots quit that by the end of 1998, half the pilots in the average squadron were new.[68] Clearly, without firing a shot, Saddam Hussein has inflicted serious damage on American forces.

We can be sure about this. The Thousand Year War between the Islamic world and the West is not about to end any time soon. I think there's a high probability of a secret deal between the Iraqi and Iranian regimes. They hate each other but they hate us more. After U.S. forces are tied up in the Balkans or elsewhere, Iranians will foment a revolution

---

[68] Defense News, November 2-8, 1998, p.7.

in Saudi Arabia. Then Iraq will take Kuwait and Iran will take Saudi Arabia, and the price of oil will hit $100 per barrel.

That's in the long run. For the short run, it's impossible to predict.

Two points to keep in mind. First, Iraq is an artificial country cobbled together by the British in the 1920s. It consists of more than a dozen ethnic groups who fought continually until Saddam came to power.

Saddam is the only person who has ever been brutal enough to control these bellicose groups, and if he goes, Iraq is likely to become another Yugoslavia. I think that after getting into the 1990-91 war, U.S. officials learned this, which is another reason President Bush gave up trying to eliminate Saddam.

Look at a map. Iraq contains ten percent of the total world oil supply and it is surrounded by tyrannical regimes — Syria, Iran, Turkey, Kuwait, Saudi Arabia and Jordan. To eliminate Saddam would be to invite chaos in Iraq, and to create the temptation for these regimes to invade and try to grab the oil. In other words, to eliminate Saddam is to set the stage for a massive Mideast oil war.

The other point is that Arab governments do not represent the Arab people. All 22 Arab governments are dictatorships. When U.S. officials speak of their Arab allies, they are referring only to the ruling elites, not the Arab people. All these tyrants worry about rebellion and assassination.

In short, that part of the world is a tinderbox soaked in oil.

I suspect that Saddam still plans to lure the U.S. government into an endless guerrilla war. If he can do it, it really will be the "Mother of all Battles." He will go down in Arab history as one of the great Arab leaders.

My long-term forecast: the whole oil corridor including the Persian Gulf will be swept by war and there's nothing anyone can do to prevent it. I wish I could say when it will happen but there's no way to know. All we can be certain about is that the stage is set.

Questions to ponder: Saddam has rebuilt his forces, has he also purchased a supply of nuclear weapons from smugglers in the former USSR? A supply of germ weapons? Has Iran? Syria? Libya?

And, what kind of superpower "leaders" do we have to handle these new threats?

Here may be the most important point to remember about Iraq. If Saddam Hussein is eliminated, this is likely to lead to a Yugoslavia in the center of the oil corridor.

Chaostan
(pronounced Chaos-tan)

Extracted from
Richard Maybury's Early Warning Report Newsletter

The world has entered another period of major upheaval. Like the Roman empire, the Soviet empire is splintering into hundreds of tiny feudal states ruled by independent warlords. These warlords can be expected to use nuclear, chemical and biological weapons on each other. I call the affected area Chaostan (pronounced Chaos-tan) meaning the land of the Great Chaos. It comprises roughly the area from the Arctic Ocean to the Indian Ocean and Poland to the Pacific, plus north Africa.

Chaostan is the most important area that never developed legal systems based on the two laws that make civilization possible: (1) do all you have agreed to do and (2) do not encroach on other persons or their property. The first is the basis of contract law, the second is the basis of tort law and some criminal law.

These two laws, common to all religions, are ethical bedrock. They were the basis of the old British Common Law, on which the American founders based The Declaration of Independence, Constitution and Bill of Rights.

In the absence of these laws, the only possibilities are tyranny or chaos. Genuine liberty and free markets are not an option.

For centuries, Chaostan and especially Russia have had tyranny. Now the area is deeply into chaos. At the start of 1999, no less than 24 wars were raging in Chaostan.

I think chaos is more frightening than tyranny, so these hundreds of millions of people will soon be begging for a return to tyranny, as the Germans were in the 1930s.

Chaostan is headed for a lot more war, and the war will affect the world economy and our investments profoundly.

It will all go the way of Yugoslavia. This great war is likely to be on the scale of the First World War, not as bad as the Second World War. However, like the Second World War, which began not in 1941 but in 1931 with Japan's invasion of Manchuria, and 1935 with Italy's invasion of Ethiopia, this war is beginning slowly and is not yet recognized for what it is.

It will be in two theaters. The northern theater will be the free-for-all among the feudal warlords, and between warlords and Moscow fascists. The southern theater will be the Islamic world vs. the West.

Until the U.S. is fully involved, America will be a haven for flight capital. The dollar and U.S. investments will continue benefiting from the influx of money from Chaostan.

After the U.S. is fully involved, taxes and inflation will be crushing; money will flee America to neutral nations such as Switzerland and New Zealand, and into precious metals, commodities and numismatics.

U.S. troops are already operating under combat conditions in two parts of Chaostan: Iraq and the Balkans.

Why is there so much fear, paranoia and hate in Chaostan?

America's own history sheds some light on it.

Some Southerners were furious about the outcome of the Civil War. They could not get revenge against the federal government, so many vented their rage on newly freed Blacks.

Blacks got caught in the crossfire between North and South, and many developed a mighty hatred of whites.

One consequence has been the race riots that periodically burn our cities. California's Watts riot and Rodney King riot were the direct result of a war that began more than a century ago and 2,300 miles away.

Take America's ethnic problems, multiply by several thousand, and you have Chaostan.

America's troubled ethnic groups number no more than a dozen.[69] Russia alone has 250, and the total for all Chaostan must be a thousand or more.

When America's ethnic groups fight, they use pistols and Uzis. In Chaostan they use howitzers, helicopter gunships and guided missiles.

---

[69] America has hundreds of ethnic groups but, unlike those of Chaostan, most are not fractious.

America as a country has been around for only about 200 years. Civilization in Chaostan goes back to Biblical times.[70] This means these hundreds of ethnic groups are carrying around thousands of years of grudges. They hate each other with a fury no American will ever understand.

It is not much of an exaggeration to say that even if you lived twenty years in a village in Chaostan, you would not understand much more than that village. To understand the village down the road, you would need to live twenty years there, for each village is a different country with different loves, hates, fears and loyalties.

Feelings are so old, intense and complicated that the western hemisphere has never experienced anything like the conflicts Chaostan has. In a single battle, at Stalingrad in World War II, more people were killed than America has lost in all the wars it has ever fought.

The Euro-Asian desire to exterminate one's neighbors grew to its present extremes during the Middle Ages. This was mostly the work of one man, Genghis Kahn.

Genghis was born in Mongolia around 1162. That's just yesterday in a part of the world that goes back so many thousands of years. To understand the powerful forces affecting your investments, you must understand what Genghis Kahn did. He was the most successful homicidal maniac in history and one of the very few ever to out-Roman the Romans.

Genghis Kahn was the consummate Mongol. While still a boy he killed his half-brother for stealing a fish. That's the kind of people who lived in Asia in those days. It was a

---

[70] The oldest known city in Chaostan is Jericho, which was established around 10,000 BC, according to the Grolier Encyclopedia.

harsh place, if the environment didn't get you another Mongol would; only the most brutal survived.

As a young man, Genghis Kahn began the conquest of other Mongol tribes, and eventually subjugated and "united" them all under his rule.

He did this by perfecting what would someday be called the blitzkrieg (lightning war). The idea of the blitzkrieg is to attack swiftly from over the horizon, hitting the enemy with sudden and overwhelming force before he realizes what is happening.

In World War II, the progress of mechanized armies was considered satisfactory if the rate of advance was 11 miles per day. Genghis Kahn's cavalry sweeping across the Asian steppes could advance at 70 miles per day, and his best units at 120.

In one campaign against Europe, the Mongol cavalry covered 8,000 miles.

Genghis Kahn was the only person ever to conduct a successful winter invasion of Russia.

Another factor that made the Mongols stand out as an unspeakable terror was their nomadic heritage. With little interest in owning land itself, they wanted only what was portable. This meant primarily food, horses and women; everything and everyone else was destroyed. Kiev in Ukraine, for instance, was completely leveled. Today we have only legends of cities in Asia that had been thriving commercial centers. We don't know where they were, Mongols demolished them so thoroughly that archeologists cannot find them. We do know the entire civilization of Xi Xia was erased.

Mongols, bred under some of the harshest conditions on earth, were the most vicious warriors in history. A kidnapped woman would be made the "wife" of her abductor. Said

Genghis Kahn, "The greatest pleasure is to vanquish your enemies and chase them before you, to rob them of their wealth and see those dear to them bathed in tears, to ride their horses and clasp to your bosom their wives and daughters."

Their systematic rape spread their DNA throughout most of Asia and east Europe. The significance of this depends on your stand in the nature vs. nurture debate, but we can safely assume Mongol DNA has not contributed much to feelings of pacifism.

Mongols ruled Russia for two centuries, and Russians have never forgotten it. Today Russians still live in fear of an unstoppable horde appearing on their horizon.

The origin of the word horde is, a tribe of Mongols.

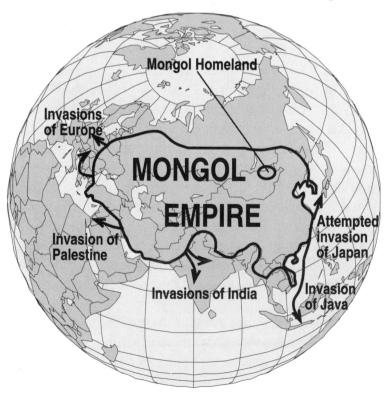

Follow this on a globe, comparing the size of the areas
to the size of the U.S. In 1211, the Mongol army pierced the
Great Wall of China. Marauding across China for 23 years,
they eventually conquered the whole country and most of
Vietnam.

The Mongol Empire eventually became the largest land
empire ever known. It stretched 2,000 miles from the Ural
Mountains to the Arabian Sea, and 5,000 miles from Poland
to Vietnam.

From China they launched a seaborne invasion of Java,
an amazing 2,000 miles to the south.

They also tried to take Japan, and nearly succeeded. A
typhoon sank 4,000 of their ships. The Japanese called the
typhoon the Kamikaze, meaning Divine Wind — the name
that would someday be used for Japanese suicide planes, in
World War II.

The Mongols commonly left in their wake body counts
of over 100,000. We don't know the total they killed, but it
was certainly millions. The horror lives today. When NA-
TIONAL GEOGRAPHIC editor Mike Edwards visited Afghanistan
he found that, "even after 750 years people spoke of the
Mongol rampage in voices tinged with apoplexy, as if it had
happened yesterday."

Think about it. What could scare you so badly that 750
years from now your descendants will be telling stories
about how awful it was?

At the Hungarian town of Muhi you can see a memorial to
the 60,000 townspeople killed by the Mongols in 1241.

In Krakow, Poland, I heard a trumpeter atop St. Mary's
church sound the alarm that was given 756 years before to
warn of the approaching Mongols. The trumpeter blows the
horn *every hour of every day*, as a reminder.

Thanks to the Mongols, the fear of invasion lurks always just beneath the surface everywhere in Europe and Asia. Russians see Moslems as Mongols, Moslems see Russians as Mongols, and West Europeans see both as Mongols.

The Islamic world tends to be even more paranoid because in the same period that Moslems were attacked by Mongols from the east they were attacked by European Crusaders from the west.

The Europeans were almost as crazy as the Mongols. French chronicler Radulph of Caen wrote, "In Ma'arra our troops boiled pagan [Moslem] adults in cooking pots; they impaled children on spits and devoured them grilled."[71]

French troops wrote a letter to the Pope saying they killed and ate children because they had run out of food,[72] but whatever the reason, it was an effective terror tactic. Moslems were as scared of the Europeans as they were of the Mongols, and the French were commonly referred to as "cannibals." Today, the medieval Moslem word for the French, the Franj, is still used by Arabs to refer to all Europeans and it still evokes the memory of what the French Crusaders did.

Sandwiched between crazy Mongols from the east and crazy Europeans from the west, Moslems were about as frightened as it was possible to be, and they still retain that fear of foreign invasion.

Again, to inhabitants of the Mideast, whose history goes back many thousands of years, a war in the Middle Ages was just yesterday, the wounds are still fresh.

---

[71] THE CRUSADES THROUGH ARAB EYES, by Amin Maalouf, Schocken Books, New York, 1984, p.39.
[72] Ibid.

In the 1990-91 war between Saddam Hussein and George Bush, Moslem newspapers sympathetic to the Iraqis began referring to the Americans and Europeans as Crusaders. After the "highway of death" photos appeared on TV, Moslems tagged us with the only label worse than Crusaders — Mongols. That was when I knew George Bush would have to either quit the war and pull out of Iraq or prepare to fight the whole Moslem world. If he pulled out, the price of oil would fall back to its pre-war level; if he stayed in, it would go through $100.

The unfinished Iraq-Kuwait war shows that events of seven centuries ago — the Mongol invasions and the fears they evoke — are still very much in play today and they have a big effect on our investments.

The Islamic world's fear of another invasion by bloodthirsty lunatics from Europe is entirely understandable. The Mongol slaughter was seven centuries ago, but the most recent European slaughter was in the 1920s and '30s when the Soviet Socialists murdered millions of Moslems in conquering Kazakhstan, Uzbekistan, Turkmenistan, Kirgizstan, Tajikistan and Azerbaijan.

This is why I am certain that U.S. meddling in that part of the world cannot lead to anything good. Few Americans can understand how those people feel, or why they are so inclined to shoot first and ask questions later. How many Americans know anything about Genghis Kahn?

There is nothing we can do about it except get neutral and stay that way, but the White House has no such intention.

Thousands of Countries

The only natural countries in Chaostan are Greece, Egypt, Turkey, Persia (Iran) and perhaps China. Within each of these lands most of the inhabitants share common languages, religions, art and political history.

Except for these, all the countries of Chaostan are artificial, created by the Europeans for the convenience of the Europeans during their conquest of the world. For a dramatic picture of this process, see the Centennia® program by Clockwork Software (distributed by Bluestocking Press). Pay particular attention to the drawing of borders in the Mideast in the period just after World War I.

Perhaps the best way to understand Chaostan is to make a map of the area and include no borders, just the cities, towns and villages. Each of these thousands of cities, towns and villages is a separate country, and not many are close friends with their neighbors. Although there are exceptions, what you see in the Balkans is typical of all of Chaostan, and has been for thousands of years.

Loose Cannons

The term loose cannon comes from the sailing ship era when artillery was carried on the decks. If a cannon broke loose during a storm, it would roll wildly, demolishing the ship.

The main point is that in a storm you do not know what a loose cannon will do, you know only that it will be awful.

In 1997, the world economy sailed into a big storm. The storm began in Chaostan.

Here are some of the worst of Chaostan's loose cannons. As we go through the list you will want to follow on a globe or world map.

Loose Cannon: Turkey

Extracted from
Richard Maybury's Early Warning Report Newsletter

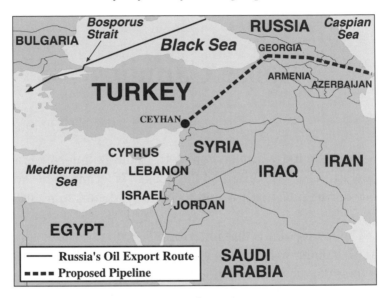

Knowledge is good. Understanding is better. Few governments mind if their people have knowledge as long as the people do not have understanding.

In America we have been taught to have a Eurocentric view of the world. News reporters attended the same schools as you and I, so when they report on international events they usually concentrate on Europe, primarily England, France, Germany and Russia.

Few Americans realize that the most important geographic position on the globe is held by Turkey, and Turkey is likely to be either the spark or one of the most important ingredients in whatever explosions happen in the new decade. If you want to understand what is coming, understand Turkey.

On October 25, 1998 Turkey's foreign minister made a crucially important announcement, and I suspect you heard nothing about it. He announced that the Turks will limit oil tanker traffic through the Bosporus Strait. He said Turkey will do whatever it can "to stop the Bosporus from becoming an oil pipeline," from the Caspian oil fields.

Here's the story. I suggest you follow on a globe or world map.

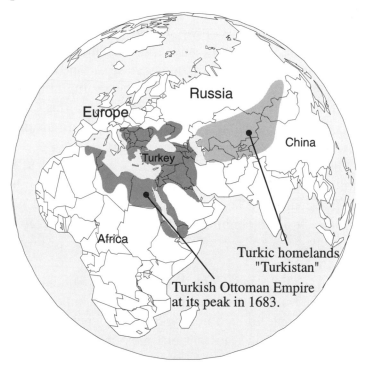

An Islamic nation on the frontier between Europe and the Islamic world, Turkey controls the Bosporus Strait, which means it controls Russia's only route to the Mediterranean. For centuries, whatever access Russians have had to warm water ports has been at the whim of the Turks.

Russians are light-skinned Christians and Turks are dark-skinned Moslems. The Black Sea is a cauldron in which Turks and Russians mix religious bigotry, racial bigotry, economic leverage and military control. Theirs is one of the oldest and most intense hatreds in history.

At its peak, the Turks' Ottoman civilization was so vast you could travel from Austria to the Pacific speaking only Turkic. And, you still can, the Ottoman empire is gone but Turkish culture remains widespread.

The Turks' deepest penetration into Europe was to Vienna in 1529. Hatred and fear of Turks from these medieval wars remains so strong in east Europe that battle monuments about the Turkic wars have been built inside the churches, and guides tell visitors hair raising stories so vivid you'd think a Turkish army is still camped just outside the walls. Europeans are very big on grudges.

The first major defeat of the Turks was at the battle of Lepanto in Greece in 1571 when their fleet was sunk by a Christian coalition. Their final defeat came in World War I when the Ottoman Empire was dismantled and Turkey was relegated to backwater status along with the rest of the Islamic world.

Then, during the Cold War (1945-1990) the Turks' unique geographic position made them so important they enjoyed a simple foreign policy situation: they were safely ensconced in NATO, ancient enemies of Russia and aloof from the rest of the Islamic world.

In the 1990s, NATO and the Kremlin became allies, with NATO giving money and military training to the Kremlin. This upset the Turkish applecart. Turks found themselves in the strange and uncomfortable position of being the odd man out, the party pooper who would not kiss and make up with the Russians.

With Cold War terrors receding, and the need for close ties to NATO disappearing, Turks began rediscovering their ancient linchpin situation. They share borders with Bulgaria, Greece, Georgia, Armenia, Iraq, Iran and Syria, and are Black Sea neighbors of Romania, Moldova and Ukraine.

Their ethnic roots are in Central Asia, where most of the population is Turkic, and Turkey adjoins the bloody Caucasus and Balkan areas.

In short, no other nation has so many opportunities to make trouble or so many reasons for paranoia.

Entirely missed by the mainstream media is the significance of the Turks' moves in the Iraq-Kuwait war. Joining George Bush against Saddam Hussein, the Turks closed Iraq's oil pipeline. Most of the Islamic world stayed neutral or rooted for Iraq, so the Turks burned a lot of bridges by siding with the Christian West.

What did they get in return? A warm thank you and the polite but firm notification that they were not light-skinned enough or Christian enough to be full and equal members of the European economy.

This did not make a good impression on them.

Insulted, stabbed in the back and spurned by the Europeans, the Turks began to reawaken their Ottoman heritage including an appreciation for their control of the Bosporus Strait.

With the collapse of the Soviet empire, the Caspian oil became a political football. Greedy for taxes they expect to collect from the oil, Russians want the oil exported through pipelines over their territory to the Black Sea and out the Bosporus.

Turks want the pipelines to bypass Russia and go across Turkey to the Mediterranean at the city of Ceyhan.

The key is the Bosporus. The Russians need access to it desperately, or they cannot get the oil out.

Despite already being the largest military power in the Islamic world, the Turks in the 1990s went on a weapons buying spree. Said Turkish Defense Minister Ismet Sezgin, "We are surrounded by instability and risks, particularly in the Middle East. ... Despite the Dayton accord, a lasting peace has yet to be constructed in Bosnia-Herzegovina. This is a potential source of unrest that is likely to spill into other Balkan countries. ... We are giving priority to the purchase of frigates, submarines, tanks, armored communication vehicles, tanker and light transport aircraft, attack helicopter production, midrange missiles, and command, control and communications systems."[73]

Here's a mystery. In 1997, DEFENSE NEWS reported that the U.S. government was donating seven tanker aircraft to Turkey's air force. These tankers are for mid-air refueling, to make long-range strikes possible. Why are U.S. officials giving the Turks the ability to hit targets distant from Turkey, and what are those targets?

Keep an eye on Turkey.

---

[73] DEFENSE NEWS, Oct 6-12, 1997, p.30

Loose Cannon: Greece

Extracted from
Richard Maybury's Early Warning Report Newsletter

To understand Chaostan, realize that the seven decades between 1920 and 1990 when the Soviet empire dominated the region were an aberration. Soviet tyranny suppressed the hundreds of nations and ethnic groups who have always fought each other, and kept them quiet, or at least quiet compared to their long, bloody history.

It took the Russians until 1952, when the last pockets of Ukrainian resistance were destroyed, to consolidate their hold on the region.

The hundreds of ethnic groups in Chaostan have always hated and fought each other. Since the beginning of history until 1920 the area was a vast sea of blood and destruction. Then, for 70 years the Soviet government sat on Chaostan like a lid on a pressure cooker. Now the lid is gone and the explosion has begun. The area is returning to its original condition of war and poverty.

Soviet tyranny controlled the hundreds of feuding groups but did not get them to kiss and make up. During the roughly 40-year period of comparative calm between 1950 and 1990, which I call the Great Intermission, the hatreds and grudges festered and grew.

During the 1990s as the mainstream press cheered the new "post-Soviet era of peace," no less than 24 wars broke out in Chaostan.

One of the strangest marriages during the Great Intermission was that of Turkey and Greece. Inhabitants of Greece and Turkey have hated and fought each other at least since the Trojan War in 1200 BC. But, during the Great Intermission, fearful of the Soviet empire, these ancient enemies joined NATO and became allies.

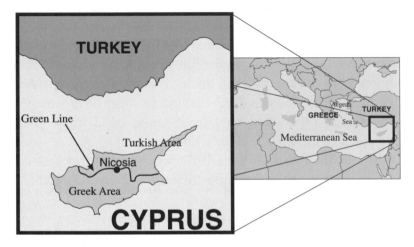

Now that they no longer fear Soviet invasion, they, like dozens of other groups in Chaostan, are returning to their old ways. Trouble is brewing between Greece and Turkey. In early 1998 they almost went to war over a tiny, uninhabited island in the Aegean.

Greeks and Turks today remain prisoners of their history. Turks originally moved west from the Altai Mountains in east Asia. Greeks came east from Greece, and in the Middle Ages the two collided in what was then called Anatolia, now Turkey. Today Turks are Moslem and Greeks are Eastern Orthodox Christian, the perfect mix for an endless feud.

By 1639, Turks had overrun all the Aegean and the Balkan peninsula including Greece. They pushed the Greeks out of Turkey but the Greeks fought back and by 1920 had regained nearly all the Aegean islands, many of which are less than ten miles from the Turkish coast.

Under international law these islands give Greeks exclusive economic rights in most of the Aegean, and severely restrict the Turk's territorial waters. If there was ever a marriage made in hell, the Greek and Turk sharing of the Aegean is it.

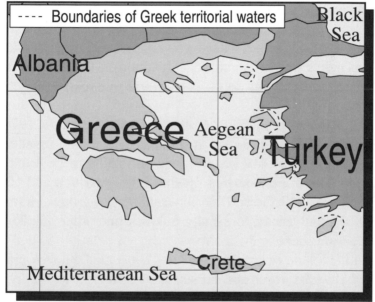

Incidentally, this dispute is typical of all Chaostan. There is hardly a national border anywhere in Chaostan that is more than a century old, and nearly all the hundreds of ethnic groups over there are convinced they have the right to retake territory owned by their ancestors.

In summary, Turks vs. Greeks is one of the world's great historic feuds. Inviting them both into NATO was about as smart as inviting the Hatfields and McCoys to the same party. NATO is required to come to the aid of whichever one is attacked, so both know that the one who is first to convincingly fake an attack by the other is the one that will receive NATO help. They are now squabbling over Cyprus.

Greeks settled on Cyprus around 1400 BC and briefly took control in 391 BC. Then the Persians took it, then the Romans and Byzantines, followed by England's Crusaders in 1191. Turks took it in 1571.

In 1878, the Turks agreed to let the British back, in exchange for help against Russia.

In 1914, in typical British fashion, the British annexed Cyprus, which did not make a good impression on the Turks. The Greeks on the island began clamoring for union with Greece, and that made an even worse impression on the Turks.

Today Cyprus is 77% Greek and 18% Turk. In 1974, fearing Greece was about to annex the island, Turkey invaded, leading to a split. Turkey has the north and Greece has the south. The Turks declared independence in 1983, and UN troops patrol the Green Line between the two groups. In the 1990s, both were buying tanks, missiles and other weapons at a furious pace.

Like all the other bloodshed in Chaostan, the developing war between Greece and Turkey is a horribly insane revival of past wars.

Loose Cannon: Iran

Extracted from
Richard Maybury's Early Warning Report Newsletter

In 1997, the mainstream press fell all over themselves welcoming Iranian president Khatami's invitation to be friends. Naive.

Many people in Iran, and throughout the Mideast, admire America and like Americans. But they hate and fear the U.S. government. One of the many reasons is that for 26 years the U.S. government backed the Shah and his secret police, who tortured and murdered thousands. The U.S. government equipped and trained the Iranian army that kept these cutthroats in power.

If someone tortured to death a member of your family, would you say, hey, no problem, let bygones be bygones, let's be friends.

Some might secretly look for ways to make the guilty party pay — and pay and pay — and to give the guilty party a false sense of security so that he could be hit when his guard is down.

Believe it, the war between Iran and the U.S. government has barely begun. It's the latest chapter in the endless conflict between Iran and the West that began 23 centuries ago. That's right, this is still Rome vs. Persia.

If you haven't yet read it, go to a bookstore and get Larry Bond's novel THE ENEMY WITHIN, it's prophetic.

Bond offers a stunning insight. In the 1990s, the Bush-Clinton arms embargo against Moslems in the Balkans got a lot of innocent Moslem men, women and children killed by the better-armed Serbs. Let me emphasize, children. Killed.

The embargo created for America a lot more "terrorist" enemies. Bond's point is that Balkan Moslems are European slavs, not Middle Easterners. Many have blond hair and blue eyes, and would have no trouble blending into American society. Until recently, the U.S. government's Islamic enemies had trouble infiltrating America, most of their "terrorist" warriors had Middle Eastern appearances.

Are you beginning to wonder who duped Timothy McVeigh into parking the truck in front of a day care center? Children. Killed.

The plot of Bond's THE ENEMY WITHIN is not just plausible, it's probable. For 23 centuries, Europeans and Iranians have hated each other. In the 1950s, the U.S. government stepped in for the Europeans. Political power corrupts both the morals and the judgment.

Nothing is likely to affect oil prices as much as the ongoing war between Iran and the White House.

THE ENEMY WITHIN contains too much Rambo for my taste, and the ending is a chapter from POLLYANNA compared to the big war that's likely, but these are my only serious criticisms.

To give you the necessary background to appreciate the book, here is a chronology of the ancient vendetta between Islamic world and the West, with emphasis on Persia. This chronology is partial. For a much more complete record, see the Centennia® program by Clockwork Software. Please keep this on file, you will want to refer back to it as events unfold in the Persian Gulf over the next few years.

Remember, Iran is Persia, and the Persian Gulf is called the Persian Gulf because it has always belonged to Persia. To keep this chronology as clear as possible, it refers to Persia not Iran.

331 BC	Europe's Alexander the Great invades and conquers Persia. This begins 23 centuries of conflict between Europe and Persia.
614	Jerusalem taken by Persians
638	Jerusalem taken by Arab Moslems
circa 970	Emperors Nicephorus Phocas and John Zimisces attack Moslems in the area which is now Turkey.
1095-circa 1300	Crusades
1090	Persians begin developing the most effective covert warfare force ever known, the Assassins. European rulers terrorized, some killed.
1602-1798	East Indies (Indonesia) conquered by Dutch
1664	Persians and Russians at war
1722	Persians and Russians at war again
1801-15	Barbary Wars (the "Shores of Tripoli"). U.S. officials deceived into abandoning neutrality and siding with Europeans in their ancient war against Moslems. *This will be the first case of the U.S. fighting the Europeans' wars for them.*

1820	Oman and Qatar under British control
1830-57	Algeria conquered by French
1834-59	Caucasus conquered by Russia
1839	Aden taken by Britain
1873-87	Uzbekistan conquered by Russia
1882	Egypt conquered by British
1885-90	Eritrea conquered by Italy
1898	Sudan conquered by Britain
1900	Chad conquered by French
1909-10	Russians and British invade Persia

Saladin is the greatly admired Moslem leader who threw the Crusaders out of the Holy Land during the Middle Ages. In 1920, when French general Gouraud entered Damascus after the battle of Maissaloun, one of the first things he did was visit the tomb of Saladin. He knocked on the door and said, "Saladin, listen, we have returned."[74]

[74] MILITANT ISLAM, by G.H. Jansen, Harper & Row, NY, 1979, p.66

1941	Russians and British invade Persia again.
1946	Russians withdraw from Persia, leaving British with control of Persian oil.
1951	Mossadegh elected Persian premier on the promise to end British control of the oil.
1953	CIA and British MI-6 help overthrow Mossadegh, install Shah as a U.S. puppet dictator. U.S. is now Europe's proxy in the Persian Gulf.
1953-79	U.S. provides Shah's troops and secret police with weapons and training. Thousands tortured and killed by secret police. Persians living in Europe beg U.S. officials to stop helping the Shah. Yet, during 26 years of terror, no U.S. official utters one word of apology to Persians. Persians develop an underground Islamic movement against the Shah and "the Great Satan" America. Friends and relatives of the Shah's victims begin refining covert warfare skills handed down over eight centuries.
1979	Revolution. Shah overthrown. Still, no U.S. apology to Persians. 52 Americans held hostage 444 days. This begins the war between Persia and the U.S.

1983	U.S. sides with Christians in Lebanon. U.S. warships shell Islamic villages. "Terrorists," probably backed by Persia, retaliate by blowing up Marine barracks, killing 241 Marines.
1984	Anti-ship mines secretly planted in Red Sea damage at least 16 ships. Did Persia do it?
1985	CIA-backed group uses car bomb on Islamic leader in Lebanon; 80 killed.
1987	Allied with Saddam Hussein in his war against Persia, U.S. Navy battles Persian navy; destroys Persian oil platforms.
1988	U.S. cruiser Vincennes in Persian Gulf shoots down Persian airliner, killing 290.
1991	Persia buys Chinese technology for enriching uranium for nuclear weapons.
1992	Reliable reports of Persia buying three Soviet nuclear weapons from Kazakhstan, and counterfeiting U.S. dollars. Persia begins buying super-quiet Russian Kilo class submarines.

"I have always given as my decided opinion that no nation had a right to intermeddle in the internal concerns of another."

George Washington, 1796

1993   World Trade Center blast. Also, a gun-
man of Middle Eastern appearance
shoots five people entering CIA headquarters parking lot.

1994   Persian Revolutionary Guards meet
with Islamic activists in Latin America.
Twelve Russian army officers with
nuclear weapons expertise are known to
be working in Persia.

1995   U.S. levies trade embargo against Persia. Persia places artillery, poison gas
and anti-ship missiles around the Strait
of Hormuz. Israeli officials say Persia's
nuclear arsenal will be active within
five years.

1996   U.S. Congress budgets $18 million to
overthrow Persia's government. Eight
months later, a blast in Saudi Arabia
kills 19 Americans.

1997   Mideast expert Robert Kaplan writes
that Persia has "a shop-till-you-drop
policy regarding nuclear and chemical
weapons."

> *"Whatever it is that the government does, sensible Ameri-*
> *cans would prefer that the government do it to somebody else.*
> *This is the idea behind foreign policy."*
>
> P.J. O'Rourke, PARLIAMENT OF WHORES, *1991*

How many investors realize that one of the most important forces affecting their investments is Alexander the Great?

> *"How soon will the explosion in the Middle East come? The signs are everywhere, even if they are largely ignored in the West."*
>
> Robert Fisk
> THE INDEPENDENT, London
> April 1, 1997

You can see why the FBI can never be very good at anticipating terrorist attacks until they begin analyzing U.S. foreign policy and studying the history of the countries in which U.S. officials meddle.

Now you are ready for THE ENEMY WITHIN. As you read, keep reminding yourself of Timothy McVeigh and Iran's "moderate" president Mohammed Khatami. And, warn everyone you care about.

Loose Cannon: Iraq

Extracted from
Richard Maybury's Early Warning Report Newsletter

One of the biggest loose cannons, Iraq, held center stage all during the 1990s, so let's take a more in-depth look at it.

Let's also keep things in perspective. Saddam Hussein is a brutal gangster but he is far from another Hitler. Among Asian rulers he is no worse than average.

If we judge by the body count, Saddam Hussein is in the same league as Boris Yeltsin, and the Clinton administration formed an *alliance* with Yeltsin.

Yeltsin, you may remember, was a high official in the Communist Party and buddy of Gorbachev when Russians were slaughtering Afghans. He was president for the war in Tajikistan and the slaughter of the Chechens, and during most of Russia's **Machiavellian** tactics in the bloody Caucasus wars. Yeltsin talked freedom but shot real bullets.

Americans do not understand how depressingly average Hussein is because they do not appreciate how wonderful America is or how awful most of the rest of the world is.

For example, in America the enslavement of African blacks was a horror, and in the 134 years since slavery was abolished, many blacks have been treated almost as badly. Yet, have you ever heard a black person say he wishes his ancestors had escaped the slavers (meaning he would have been born in Africa)?

That's how awful Africa is. Most of the rest of the world isn't a lot better.

In the long list of European, Asian and African tyrants —

Julius Caesar, Genghis Khan, Attila the Hun, Mao and all the rest — Saddam Hussein is a featherweight. Given his lifetime rap sheet, he'd need to live 976 years to kill as many people as Hitler, 1,037 years to kill as many as Tamerlane, 2,135 years to kill as many as socialist Mao, and 3,294 years to kill as many as socialist Stalin.

So why all this fuss over Saddam?

Politicians acquire power by promising to defend us against threats. Any threat will do — communism, unemployment, global warming, global cooling, global freeze drying. Most of politics is about the cultivation of threats. A healthy government is one with a big inventory of threats, and a threat shortage is a disaster to be avoided at all costs.

I think that after the Soviet empire fell apart, Washington needed a new threat, and Saddam Hussein got the job.

Until then he was an ally. Remember the Iran-Iraq war? In 1980, Saddam invaded Iran. All during that eight-year war, as long as he was murdering Iranians — which included using nerve gas on them — he was a good guy helped by both the Kremlin and the White House.

Iranians, incidentally, will not soon forget this.

Saddam's good guy status was so firm that, in 1987, when one of his planes (accidentally?) fired an Exocet missile into the USS Stark killing 37 Americans, he was given a pass. Hey, no problem, just be more careful next time. Such courtesies are extended only to allies as close as Britain or Canada.

Then in 1990, the Kuwaitis were stealing Iraq's oil,[75] and George Bush backed his cronies the Kuwaitis. Never have I seen such an effective job of turning an ally into an enemy.

---

[75] MY AMERICAN JOURNEY by Colin Powell, 1995, p.459-460, and EARLY WARNING REPORT, 1/98, p.1.

Saddam is still an amateur but his performance in the Iran-Iraq war shows potential. If President Clinton, NATO and the UN scrimmage with him often enough, they'll train him right into the pros. Is this their plan?

Also bear in mind that Saddam does not act alone. The whole Iraqi Baathist regime is his type of people, and they hate the West as much as he does. Get rid of him and he might be replaced by someone worse.

What about Saddam's weapons of mass destruction? All the New Axis states either have them or can easily get them, they sell them to each other. This includes Iran, and Iran is the real 400-pound gorilla of the Persian Gulf.

A key point: remember Lebanon. Like Iraq, it was a collection of groups cobbled together by outsiders, and after World War II, became independent. In 1975, the Lebanese central government lost control and the Lebanese Civil War broke out. The bloody chaos lasted 15 years. At one point in 1983, I counted no less than 50 groups fighting to be the new government.

> *"The Islamic world this month united itself behind, of all persons, Saddam Hussein, or at least united against his adversaries in Washington. Saddam's crimes are evident enough to the world, but it is also evident that he scored a victory over Bill Clinton by recovering, by proxy at least, a part of his country that had been declared off limits to him. To the West, Saddam is an unlikely hero, but to peoples who count themselves as the world's underdogs, any victory of one of their own is better than none at all."*
>
> *George Melloan*
> WALL STREET JOURNAL, *9/16/96*

Also remember what happened in Yugoslavia. This again was an artificial country cobbled together from diverse groups of enemies. Tito was the only person ruthless enough to keep them from fighting, his real constitution was just six words: if you make trouble you die.

Iraq is another artificial country and Saddam Hussein is its Tito. He is the only person who has been ruthless enough to keep the many tribes from slaughtering each other.

Iraq's opposition groups number around 80. So, when Hussein goes, we can expect to see 80 groups fighting to be the new government.

This explosion will have a booster. Iraq contains 10% of the total world oil supply, and is surrounded by ruthless dictatorial regimes — the Saudis, Kuwaitis, Iranians, Turks and Syrians. All are ancient enemies, and none want the others to get Iraq's oil. When Saddam dies and Iraq's chaos erupts, these surrounding cutthroats can be expected to pounce like wolves on a wounded deer, all fighting for the choicest parts.

This is why everyone is afraid to kill Saddam, he is the only thing holding this fury in check.

The fuse on the powderkeg is already burning, one of the wolves has already begun to pounce. The Turks, who are backed by President Clinton, are building bases in northern Iraq.[76] Saddam cannot stop them, the Turks are covered by the U.S. air umbrella.

The Syrians and Iranians must be saying to themselves, we need to make a grab soon before the Turks take it all.

The coming oil war is as inevitable as anything in human affairs can be, and it is likely to be the worst oil war yet, by far. The 1991 Iraq-Kuwait war drove oil to $40, so I am sure this one, when it is fully developed, will bring at least $50.

---

[76] "Realpolitik..." WALL STREET JOURNAL, February 13, 1998

Whether the price stays there or not will depend on how much damage is done to the Kuwaiti, Saudi and Iranian oil fields. If they are demolished, I'll look for $100 or more.

Watch those Turkish bases, they could be the trigger for the catastrophe.

The only U.S. foreign policy that would be good for America is neutrality, and a readiness to pay $2.00 per gallon for gasoline. But no president in a hundred years has been willing to seriously consider neutrality — they call it isolationism — so I am convinced we are headed for the biggest war yet in the Persian Gulf.

Stay tuned, and warn everyone you care about.

Loose Cannon: Indonesia

Extracted from
Richard Maybury's Early Warning Report Newsletter

In 1993, I added Indonesia to the map of Chaostan. Now daily headlines tell you why, but they only scratch the surface. Here's the story.

In 1975, the U.S. merchant ship Mayaguez was seized by pirates in the South China sea. The crew was rescued by the U.S. Navy and Marines, 38 of whom were killed in the battle.

Why do people think piracy is a subject for cartoons and amusement park rides? Piracy means robbery, rape and murder.

In 1996, pirates stole the oil tanker Suci headed for Singapore. In 1995, in the same region they hijacked the Cypriot freighter Anna Sierra for its $5 million cargo of sugar.

Pirate attacks in the South China Sea and Indonesia are not unusual, each year dozens of vessels are hit.

For centuries, piracy was a deadly obstacle to world trade, until the U.S. and British navies undertook a massive effort to wipe it out. By 1950, the task was nearly complete. The main exception was and still is the waters around Indonesia where poverty, contempt for western governments, and a maze of thousands of islands have foiled all efforts.

Recently, as the military power of the U.S. and Britain has waned, the pirates have come back strong. Unconfirmed reports even claim pirate raids by Indonesian and Chinese naval vessels.

This is a main reason Indonesia, which entered a **depression** in 1998, has become a loose cannon. It sits astride all east-west shipping routes between Australia and the Asian mainland. Not many patches of ocean are more important. In World War II, one of Japan's first objectives was the Strait of Malacca.

Indonesia is huge, check your globe or world map, it's 3,200 miles across — the distance from Seattle to Bermuda — with 34,000 miles of coastline. It consists of 17,508 islands, about 6,000 of them inhabited. The other 11,500 offer countless hiding places for pirates, who carry rocket launchers, shoulder-launched guided missiles and other modern weapons that became available on the **black market** when the Soviet empire fell apart.

There's more. The colossus of Southeast Asia, Indonesia is the world's fourth most populous nation and largest Islamic nation, 87% of its 202 million people are Moslems. In the Iraq-Kuwait war, the Indonesian government claimed to back George Bush but the population was behind Iraq. Many influential Indonesians were schooled in Iraq.

Islam arrived in Indonesia in the 13th century. In the 16th, Europeans invaded, dragging Indonesia into the Thousand Year War between the Islamic world and Europe.

Look back over the past thousand years. It's not much of an exaggeration to say that wherever you find Moslems you find European governments trying to kill them.

Indonesia's trade routes were (and are) so important that the British, Dutch, Spanish and Portuguese not only fought the Moslems for them, they fought each other.

To this toxic heritage of piracy, religious bigotry and war, add Indonesia's more than 100 ethnic groups, none of whom have much good to say about each other, as is typical all across Chaostan.

In addition to the pirates, in 1998, Indonesia already had one guerrilla war underway, on the island of Timor, and at least two more brewing on Sumatra and Irian Jaya.

In short, Indonesia is the Balkans of the East, except that it is far bigger and more important to the world economy. To avoid these waters a ship must go around Australia, which is the size of the 48 United States.

It seems likely that Indonesia will shatter into hundreds of impoverished feudal island states hostile to the West. This will bring a plague of piracy that will either strangle trade or tie up much of the U.S. Navy, reducing the Navy's ability to protect its pet dictators in the oil-rich Persian Gulf.

The Philippines, too, is infested with Islamic guerrillas and pirates, as is the Gulf of Thailand. The U.S. government is already short of aircraft carriers, and I cannot see how the shipping lanes could be kept open with anything less than three carriers, maybe five.

The waters in and around Indonesia are likely to be highly important to the world economy and your investments, keep a close eye on them.

Loose Cannon: Russia

Extracted from
Richard Maybury's Early Warning Report Newsletter

Russia is no longer a country, it's just a place. It has splintered into hundreds of tiny feudal kingdoms ruled by mafia chiefs.

In 1998, Cox News ran a story about a shipment of wine held up by a Russian customs official demanding a $10,000 bribe. The importer said to the official, "Why would I pay you $10,000 when I could have you killed for $2,000?" The importer got his wine.

Russian ethics have become so bad the slave trade has returned. In December, 1997 in Milan, Italy, police raided an auction where Russian women were being sold at an average price of $1,000 each. Moscow and Kiev (Ukraine) are the centers of the new slave smuggling industry, reports Michael Specter of the NEW YORK TIMES.

Russian food production is a disaster. The Russian diet has gotten worse, and life expectancy for men is the worst in the industrialized world, 58 years. In the past ten years, per capita alcohol consumption has risen 600%.

On top of all this, in 1998 the Asian financial meltdown spread to Russia.

By the end of 1998, the Russian presidency, and the government as a whole, were mere figureheads with no real power left. Probably no Russian leaders could raise an army of more than a few thousand loyal troops.

If the Russian presidency goes up for grabs, keep in mind that the Russian constitution gives near dictatorial power to the president. Every mafia chief will be faced with the fact that if he does not make a grab for this power, it could fall into the hands of his enemies, who would use it to bankrupt or kill him.

To get a good feel for Russian psychology and where it is likely to lead us, get National Geographic's videotape RUSSIA'S LAST TSAR (800-552-8300). Pay close attention to the information about the Cossacks. Fiercely Christian, Cossacks were the "sword arm of the Czars" and Russia's most dedicated enemies of the Moslems. If a Russian leader can rally the Cossacks around him, that could be the beginning of one of the worst Russian vs. Moslem wars in history. Both sides have nuclear, chemical and biological weapons.

Loose Cannon: Oman

Extracted from
Richard Maybury's Early Warning Report Newsletter

Oman is the most important Arab nation of the Persian Gulf and was the first to ask for U.S. protection from Iran.

Is Oman switching sides? In an interview released January 5, 1998, the Omani Secretary-General for Foreign Affairs said, "As you look at the geopolitical situation, it is really changing. ... The threats are diminishing to Oman. ... We now have good relations with our neighbors. ... Do we have a problem with Iran to be threatened by their submarines? No we don't. Do we have territorial disputes? No." [77]

Check the map. Iran and Oman together would have a stranglehold on oil leaving the Persian Gulf.

Watch Oman.

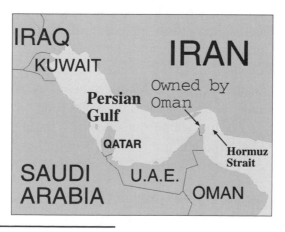

---

[77] DEFENSE NEWS, January 5-11, 1998, p.22

Loose Cannon: Kazakhstan

Extracted from
Richard Maybury's Early Warning Report Newsletter

In 1998, the mainstream press was still optimistic about the Caspian Sea area, especially Kazakhstan. The U.S. government claimed Kazakhstan had a stable government, and the place is sitting atop an ocean of oil, plus coal, gas, iron, gold and a lot of other mineral wealth.

Supposedly, all that's needed to get the oil out is several new pipelines to the Mediterranean. Azerbaijan has a lot of oil and needs a way to ship it out, too.

Turkey's regime wants the oil piped through Turkey. Turkey and Azerbaijan are some of Russia's most ancient and hated enemies. Their heritage is Moslem; Russia's is Christian.

On October 9th, 1995, President Clinton pressured the oil consortium led by Amoco and British Petroleum into a preliminary agreement to run the main pipeline through Turkey.

The U.S. government had again stuck its nose into one of the oldest and most dangerous vendettas on the planet.

Kazakhstan may be the second most hazardous place on earth (behind the Balkans) because of its history. Kazakhs are Turkic Moslem, natural allies of Turkey. All of central Asia — Kazakhstan, Uzbekistan, Turkmenistan, Kirgizstan and Tajikistan — was once called Turkistan, meaning the land of the Turks. Until the Kremlin finally conquered these people, the Czars settled their toughest troops, the Cossacks, in forts along the border with what is now Kazakhstan. This gave Kazakhstan an artificial Russian population in the north. The south remains mostly Kazakh, and Kazakhs control the government.

This north-south division is a natural setting for civil war. In the 1930s, Russian conquerors killed a million Kazakhs; their families have not forgotten.

After the Kazakhs were subdued, the Kremlin moved more slavic Christians into the area. Today, this homeland of Moslems is only 42% Kazakh, and 37% Russian, plus 5% German, 5% Ukrainian and about 100 other nationalities, none of them very friendly toward each other. Kazakhstan also has thousands of nuclear, chemical and biological weapons which the rulers swear they are deactivating. Do you believe them?

To summarize, in Kazakhstan we have great mineral wealth and many ethnic groups who until a few decades ago had been slaughtering each other for centuries. It is a potential Yugoslavia multiplied by 100, and the U.S. government cannot resist the temptation to get involved.

Question: is Central Asia developing an oil war with religious undertones or a religious war with oil undertones?

Loose Cannon: Saudi Arabia

Extracted from
Richard Maybury's Early Warning Report Newsletter

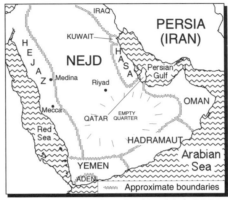

Arabian Penninsula (Arabia) 1900

Arabian Penninsula 1998

Look at a world map from the last century and you will find the Arabian peninsula labeled Arabia, not Saudi Arabia. This seems a small point but it's a key to understanding what's happening in the Persian Gulf.

Saudi Arabia is a giant desert a third the size of the U.S. but with only 19.5 million people. (The U.S. has 268 million.) Most of the Arabian peninsula is so dry and worthless that until this century few tribes bothered to draw the boundaries between their territories.

Until the early Middle Ages the peninsula was inhabited only by a few nomadic bands. Then it was gradually divided into numerous states often at war with each other. One of these was the Saud family dynasty founded in the 1400s.

In the 1500s the Turks gained control of the area along the Red Sea called the Hejaz, and in the 1800s the British took parts of Hasa and Oman along the east coast, and Aden in the southwest tip.

The wars among the tribes continued until the 1930s when ibn-Saud, backed by the British, finally conquered the other tribes. He established the state of Saudi Arabia roughly within its present boundaries. Yemen and the other small states of the Arabian peninsula are the lands ruled by tribes the Saudis did not subdue.

Why is the name Saudi Arabia so important?

It causes the misleading assumption that the Saudi family are the rightful owners of the place and the rightful representatives of the people. It's as if a Canadian family named Ferguson had conquered Canada and had the gall to rename it Ferguson Canada, and everyone in the world including the U.S. government now referred to all Canadians as Fergusons. In short, Saudi Arabia is one of the most successful hoaxes in history.

The Saudis are dictators who rule the other tribes with a heavy hand. If they didn't have all that oil, other cultures would regard them as just one more group of thugs in the same league as Qadaffi, Assad and Saddam Hussein.

For U.S. investors Saudi Arabia is one of the most important countries in the world. It is the largest oil exporter containing somewhere between 25% and 30% of the known world oil supply. When Saudi Arabia sneezes, U.S. investment markets catch pneumonia.

While we cannot be certain, it looks like a big sneeze is on the way. The exact timing is not predictable but when it happens, investors who are in the right oil stocks will profit enormously. Those who aren't will be seriously hurt.

The key point for investments is that the Saudi royal family is roundly hated by their subjects. The king and his tribe live in great opulence that provokes much jealously. Everyone knows the Saudi tribe has no more rightful claim to the oil money than any other tribe.

The Saudis have two armies so that if one revolts they can pit the other against it.

Their primary means of preventing revolts has been to spread some of the wealth around in the theory that if the population can be kept in a kind of welfare stupor like domesticated cattle, few will have the initiative to revolt. So far it has worked.

The Saudis allow no freedom of speech or press. Every non-Saudi knows that if he gets caught saying something unflattering about a member of the royal family he might vanish.

It's a big family. Ibn-Saud had 150 wives, so today a legion of 6,000 Saudi princes occupy the most important and high-paying jobs; they keep the economy in a chokehold of **nepotism**.

Political parties are not permitted. Activists are arrested and tortured including electric shock and flogging. Judges are influenced by the royal family and they can be overruled by the king.

No one in the Islamic world ever forgets that the hated Saudi conquerors sit atop 260 billion barrels of oil, and they got there with the help of one of Islam's oldest enemies, Britain. Worse, the Saudis are trying to stay there with the help of Britain's ally, the U.S. This is a time bomb that *will* go off, count on it, the only question is when.

Tensions rise a bit more each year. Despite the carloads of money earned by all that oil, the Saudis are now managing to spend it faster than they can earn it. Infrastructure goes without repairs as contractors wait months to be paid. Some neighborhoods experience frequent water cutoffs. Hospital beds are in short supply. New homes sit empty for lack of electrical service.

As the Saudi welfare state crumbles, the influence of Islamic rebels increases. Underground faxes against the royal family are widely read and discussed. Popular music has become openly antiroyal. A line in one song says, "Kings when they enter a country despoil it and make the noblest of its people the lowest."

Middle class Arabs keep mental lists of the rumored prices of each royal palace.

Jokes depict King Fahd as a witless tyrant. This is very important. The one weapon no government can stand against is ridicule. Once bureaucrats, police and troops are embarrassed to be a part of the institution, their morale drops, they quit doing their jobs, and that's the end of it. (If you really want to fight back against the ruling elite in any country, compile a list of jokes about them and pass them around.)

How hopeless is the situation? Try to imagine, the Saudis have a fourth of all the oil in the world and a population of only 19.5 million — the same as Texas — yet they spend the money so fast their government is broke.

The royal family's complete dependence on the protection of the West was demonstrated in the Iraq-Kuwait war. When the ground war began on January 16, 1991, the Saudi troops immediately abandoned their equipment and fled to take cover behind U.S. lines. A disgusted British officer said, "They bugged out."

As if all those historical and financial problems were not enough, Saudi Arabia also contains Mecca and Medina. These are Islam's two holiest cities. This means the shrines that are Islam's most sacred are under control of a regime that is widely perceived as Islam's most corrupt. A nitro and glycerine combination if there ever was one. Imagine how Catholics would feel if the Vatican were conquered and controlled by Al Capone.

A popular song in Saudi Arabia is titled "Islam vs. Christianity," and Moslems everywhere wonder which side the Saudi royal family is really on.

In 1981, President Reagan pledged U.S. protection for the Saudi regime against all enemies internal as well as external. This means, apparently, that when the Saudi rulers finally do come under attack by their own people, their dictatorship will be protected by U.S. troops.

How many U.S. troops realize what they've signed on for? How many remember it was the Saudis who led the 1973 oil embargo against the U.S.?

We can never be sure about these things but the great rebellion in Saudi Arabia may be near, due to breakthroughs in electronics.

As with all dictatorships, the primary means the Saudis use to control their people is to control the information the people receive. For years Saudi police have searched out and destroyed satellite TV dishes which receive uncensored satellite news broadcasts from abroad. But the dishes are being downsized, some now are as small as 18" in diameter and can be hidden anywhere. Also, phone line access to the Internet is fast becoming universal.

So, the new electronics combined with Saudi Arabia's deteriorating financial condition means the end of the Saudi royal family. My guess is that Iran's secret agents will continue working to foment revolution, and they will do it in a way designed to prevent U.S. intervention. The rebels will claim to be fighting for a more democratic Arabia. Once they have succeeded and are in power they will request assistance from Iran to "stabilize" Arabia. This voluntary invitation to Iran by the new "democratic" government will be an end run that will deprive the U.S. government of justification to intervene.

The new Arabian government will be, in effect, a puppet of Iran, and Iran will get **de facto** ownership of all that oil. If Iran can also take the smaller Persian Gulf oil states in the process, they will end up controlling half of all the oil in the world.

The U.S. government has little understanding of Saudi Arabia. As in Iran in the 1970s, U.S. officials deal with the English-speaking elite and get only their view of things. When the big rebellion happens, today's politicians will probably be as surprised as their predecessors were when the Shah of Iran was overthrown.

The only thing certain about Saudi Arabia is that it cannot last. Saudi Arabia *will* go back to being Arabia, and the bloody transition *will* cause oil prices to soar. When? We cannot know, human behavior is difficult to predict. We can say only that with the financial problems, the decline of the welfare handouts, and the new advances in electronics, the stage is set.

In all the Islamic world the only tribe that is despised more than the Saudis is the Kuwaitis, who also got where they are with the help of the much hated British and U.S.

I believe the forecast that makes the most sense is this: Iraq and Iran will continue working secretly to get the U.S. armed forces hopelessly tangled up in the Balkans or elsewhere. Then they will foment revolutions in Kuwait and Saudi Arabia. Iraq will take Kuwait and Iran will take the rest of the Persian Gulf plus Mecca and Medina.

Eventually — maybe immediately, maybe later — Iraqis and Iranians will fight among themselves for ownership of the whole prize, and all the Persian Gulf oil fields will go up in flames as Kuwait's did in 1991.

Generally when a government gets into the kind of trouble the Saudis have gotten themselves into, it will try to buy time by printing money. A leading indicator to watch is the value of the Saudi currency, the riyal. This is reported daily in the WALL STREET JOURNAL and other major newspapers. When you see the riyal dropping sharply, look out.

Again, the exact timing is impossible to predict. Remain watchful and warn everyone you care about.

Loose Cannon: Kurdistan

Extracted from
Richard Maybury's Early Warning Report Newsletter

When Europeans were carving the Mideast into their various empires, they had no use for Kurds, so Kurdistan was sliced up like a Christmas ham. Parts went to Iraq, Syria, Iran, Turkey and the Soviet Union.

Kurds want independence, so these governments hunt them down and kill them. During the 1990s, the government of Turkey led the hunt.

Turkey is a member of NATO. This means Turkey's Kurd-hunters are backed by the White House.

Kurds are certainly one of the most persecuted groups on the planet, and we can be confident they are getting a bit cross about it. Consider where this may lead.

The Mideast has always been a hotbed of smuggling. Kurdistan, being an outlaw area, is a spiderweb of smuggling routes.

Standard practice in Europe during the Middle Ages was for a band of thieves to claim ownership of a mountain pass. They would build a castle overlooking the pass, and demand a percentage of whatever a merchant might be transporting through the pass. The customary percentage stolen on each transit is where we get the word **customs**. Today you can still see a lot of customs castles in Italy's beautiful Brenner Pass and other parts of Europe.

In the mountainous areas of Chaostan, and especially the Mideast, this system of customs is still in operation. A guerrilla band will claim a pass and charge a tax for everything moving through it. Sometimes the tax is in the form of cash, other times a portion of whatever goods the traveler may be carrying.

If nuclear, chemical and biological weapons are moving from the former USSR into the Mideast, they are probably moving through Kurdistan. And, Kurdish groups that control the passes are undoubtedly demanding a percentage of the cargo.

Yet, the White House continues backing the Turkish Kurd-hunters on the apparent assumption no nuclear, chemical or biological weapons are in Kurdistan.

If America loses a city, one of the first groups I will suspect is Kurds. By remaining allied with Turkey, the White House is practically daring them to do it.

.."a passionate attachment of one nation for another produces a variety of evils. Sympathy for the favorite nation, facilitating the illusion of an imaginary common interest in cases where no real common interest exists, and infusing into one the enmities of the other, betrays the former into a participation in the quarrels and wars of the latter, without adequate inducement or justification. It leads also to concession to the favorite nation of privileges denied to others, which is apt doubly to injure the nation making the concessions; by unnecessarily parting with what ought to have been retained; and by exciting jealousy, ill-will and a disposition to retaliate, in the parties from whom equal privileges are withheld. And it gives to ambitious, corrupted or deluded citizens (who devote themselves to the favorite nation) facility to betray, or sacrifice the interests of their own country, without odium, sometimes even with popularity .... Against the insidious wiles of foreign influence, (I conjure you to believe me fellow-citizen) the jealousy of a free people ought to be constantly awake."

— George Washington
FAREWELL ADDRESS, 1796

"I have ever deemed it fundamental for the United States never to take active part in the quarrels of Europe. Their political interests are entirely distinct from ours. Their mutual jealousies, their balance of power, their complicated alliances, their forms and principles of government, are all foreign to us. They are nations of eternal war."

— Thomas Jefferson, 1823

"Never was so much false arithmetic employed on any subject, as that which has been employed to persuade nations that it is in their interest to go to war."

— Thomas Jefferson, 1782

Richard Maybury's Newsletter

Richard Maybury ("Uncle Eric") writes an investment newsletter called EARLY WARNING REPORT. EWR is the first and only publication to report on Chaostan and its effects on the economy and your investments.

In addition to the kind of extensive historical analysis you have read in this book, EWR offers specific investment recommendations on stocks, bonds, currencies, interest rates, precious metals and more.

Most of Mr. Maybury's analysis is based on the connection between law and economics, especially the two fundamental laws and what happens when they are violated.

EARLY WARNING REPORT gives special attention to the Mideast and the Thousand Year War.

All the maps and most of the text in this book originally appeared in EARLY WARNING REPORT.

For more information see page 269.

Please Write "Uncle Eric" With Your Ideas, Questions and Concerns

Watch for future books by Richard J. Maybury. One will be answers to questions from readers. Send your questions or comments to him in care of "Uncle Eric," Bluestocking Press, P.O. Box 1014, Dept. TYW, Placerville, CA 95667-1014. All letters become property of Bluestocking Press and may be published in whole or in part without payment to the writer. Please tell us if you want your name kept confidential. Topics can include, but are not limited to economics, government, history and law.

If your letter is published in a future "Uncle Eric" book or used in a future "Uncle Eric" audiocassette tape you will receive a free autographed copy of that book or tape.

Bibliography & Suggested Reading
(Except where noted, all are suitable
for ages 14 through adult.)

• ALMANAC OF AMERICA'S WARS, by John S. Bowman, Mallard Press, Hong Kong, 1990. An excellent chronicle of the U.S. government's battles with foreigners and with its own people. Few Americans have any idea what their government has done in foreign lands.

• ARABISTS, THE, by Robert D. Kaplan, The Free Press, NY, 1993. The fascinating story of the Christian missionaries who tried to get America out of the Thousand Year War and put us on good terms with the Islamic world.

• ATLAS OF WORLD HISTORY by Noel Grove, National Geographic Society, 1997. An outstanding tour of world history with many maps and illustrations. Rare for its inclusion of economic history. Gorgeous photography. An excellent accompaniment to Centennia® (see separate listing).

• BALKAN GHOSTS, by Robert D. Kaplan, St. Martin's Press, NY, 1993. Kaplan travels in the Balkans talking with the people to learn their feelings about each other and the people in the neighboring town. Frightening.

• BEST ENEMY MONEY CAN BUY, THE, by Antony Sutton, published by Liberty House Press, MT, 1986. A record of U.S. support for the Soviet Union during the Cold War.

- CENTENNIA® by Clockwork Software, Chicago, IL (also available through Bluestocking Press). This computer program is the best tool for students of history ever created. Simple to use, it gives a moving picture and running narrative of all the border changes in Europe, the Mediterranean and Mideast from the year 1000 to today. Get the equivalent of a college degree in history on one computer disk. Ages 10 through adult.

- CRUSADES THROUGH ARAB EYES, THE, by Amin Maalouf, Shocken Books, NY, 1984. A must for students of the Thousand Year War, tells the story of the Crusades as the Arab Moslems saw it.

- DISCOVERY OF FREEDOM, THE by Rose Wilder Lane, published for Fox and Wilkes, San Francisco, CA. Traces the development of freedom from one civilization to the other throughout history.

- ENEMY WITHIN, THE by Larry Bond, Warner Books, NY, 1996. A novel about Iran retaliating against the U.S.

- ENDS OF THE EARTH, THE, by Robert Kaplan, Random House, NY, 1996. Much like BALKAN GHOSTS, Kaplan travels across Chaostan talking with the people to learn how they really feel about each other and the people in the neighboring town.

- EXTRAORDINARY POPULAR DELUSIONS AND THE MADNESS OF CROWDS by Charles Mackay, published by Crown, NY, 1980. One of the best books ever written about mob psychology, contains a detailed account of the Crusades.

- FAILURE OF AMERICA'S FOREIGN WARS, THE, by Richard M. Ebeling and Jacob G. Hornberger, Future of Freedom Foundation, Fairfax, VA, 1997. The title says it all. A non-statist look at America's wars.

- FLASHPOINTS by Robin Wright and Doyle McManus, Alfred A. Knopf, NY, 1991. A tour of the world just after the fall of the Soviet Empire to give the history of the areas most likely to bring trouble.

- INVESTMENT BIKER, by Jim Rogers, Random House, NY, 1994. Finance and economics expert Jim Rogers travels around the world on a motorcycle and gives you his observations and insights about the lands he visits. Rogers spent a lot of time in Chaostan and has much to say about it. This book is a must.

- MAINSPRING OF HUMAN PROGRESS, THE, by Henry Grady Weaver, published by The Foundation for Economic Education, Irvington-on-Hudson, New York. Excellent overview of world history. Ages 14 and up.

- MUSLIM DISCOVERY OF EUROPE, THE, by Bernard Lewis, W.W. Norton & Co., NY, 1982. After Europe's Roman Empire fell apart, Europe slid into a Dark Age so grim the continent nearly fell off the map of the world. It was much like "Darkest Africa" was regarded by Europeans in the 1800s. During the Arab-Moslem Golden Age, Moslems began to explore Europe and report on their discoveries. They referred to Europe as "The House of War."

- ONE POINT SAFE by Andrew and Leslie Cockburn, Doubleday, NY, 1997. A revealing though not very well written compilation of the evidence that nuclear weapons have been stolen from the former Soviet Union and sold into the black market, probably to groups in the Mideast.

- SACRED RAGE by Robin Wright, published by Simon & Schuster, NY, 1986. A fascinating report on the reasons why so many people in the Mideast hate the West, and what they are doing about it.

- "Tent of Saud," WORTH magazine's 11/95 article by Jim Rogers. Author of INVESTMENT BIKER, (see separate listing), Rogers explains the deteriorating condition of the oil-rich Saudi dictatorship.

- TIMES ATLAS OF WORLD HISTORY, edited by Geoffrey Barraclough, Hammond, New Jersey, 1986. An outstanding narrative of world history including plenty of highly detailed maps.

- WALL STREET JOURNAL, series of front-page articles about the Islamic world that appeared in the August 7, 10 and 11, 1987 issues. A good overview.

The World's Political Hotspots
(audio history on cassettes)
by Knowledge Products

(distributed by Bluestocking Press)

- THE MIDDLE EAST: By the end of WWII, Britain had promised control of this area to no less than three groups: two of them were Arabs and Jews. Both of these peoples claimed a long-standing right to the same piece of land, and violence was inevitable. This presentation examines how and why this land has become a virtual war zone.

- RUSSIA AND THE SOVIET UNION: The Soviet Union never was a monolith; it was a collection of nationalities, many with serious objections to union. The demise of communism holds great promise and great danger not only for former Soviets, but for everyone. These tapes examine how the region's long history led to the USSR's rise and collapse.

- THE PERSIAN GULF STATES: More than half of the world's oil comes from Persian Gulf states. Political instability and religious strife here threaten to interrupt economic routines throughout the world. Two cassettes examine the history of Persia, including Iran's attempt to westernize and the Moslem backlash against the west and against each other.

- INDIA & PAKISTAN: As one of the world's most ancient civilizations, India presents a rich mosaic of political, religious, and cultural influences. In 1947, this vast nation was split into two nations, Pakistan and India, to separate battling Hindus and Moslems; millions died. Strife and political troubles have continued throughout the region.

- THE MEDITERRANEAN BASIN: The lands surrounding the Mediterranean Sea contain some of the oldest cultures on Earth. Italy, Greece, Egypt, and other countries or Europe and North Africa have played a central role in various expanding empires — and also in shrinking fortunes. This presentation explores the broad sweep of history in one of the cradles of civilization.

- CENTRAL EUROPE: HUNGARY, YUGOSLAVIA, CZECHOSLOVAKIA: These ancient civilizations have long been dominated by empires: the Roman Empire, the Habsburg Empire (based in Austria) and, more recently, the Soviet Communists. But the decline of communism in the late twentieth century has unleashed old resentments, rivalries, and ambitions that have caused yet more war in this troubled region.

Religion

(audio cassettes)
by Knowledge Products

(distributed by Bluestocking Press)

- JUDAISM: Judaism is both a religion and a way of life. It has several major forms or traditions (Orthodox, Conservative, Reform, and Reconstructionist Judaism); it also is the parent religion of both Christianity and Islam. Jewish sacred literature preserves the ancient oral tradition through the Hebrew Bible (which Christians call the Old Testament) and other writings (in particular, the Talmud). Judaism exalts the divine gifts of the Torah, God's teaching or instruction.

- ISLAM: Islam today is a rapidly growing religion: Indonesia, the most populous Islamic land, has well over 100 million Muslims. Islam began the seventh century, and has evolved into various forms — Sunni, Shi'ah, Sufi mysticism, etc. Also described are the backgrounds and connections of related groups like the Druse, Baha'i, the Nation of Islam, and others.

- ORTHODOX AND ROMAN CATHOLIC CHRISTIANITY: These churches have their roots in first century Christianity; their basic doctrines were summarized in the great Councils of the Churches. Yet Orthodox and Catholic life have diverged through the centuries as each embraced different ideas about worship, ethics, and relations to politics and culture. Each faith remains a vital force among large bodies of followers.

Movies

- CRUSADES, THE available through the History Channel. Call 800-708-1776.

- KHARTOUM starring Charlton Heston and Laurence Olivier, 1996.

- LAWRENCE OF ARABIA starring Peter O'Toole and Omar Sharif, 1962. Seven Oscars, including Best Picture and Best Director (David Lean).

- RED CORNER, starring Richard Gere, 1997, MGM.

- ROBIN HOOD: PRINCE OF THIEVES. Starring Kevin Costner, 1991. Rated PG-13.

Mail Order Bookstores

Bluestocking Press, P.O. Box 1014, Dept. TYW, Placerville, CA 95667, 1-800-959-8586 or 1-530-621-1123.

Foundation for Economic Education, Irvington-on-Hudson, NY 10533.

Henry-Madison Research, Box 1616 TWY, Rocklin, CA 95677.

Laissez Faire Books, 942 Howard St., San Francisco, CA 94103.

The Liberator Catalog, Advocates for Self-Government, 3955 Pleasantdale Road #106A, Atlanta, GA 30340.

Liberty Tree Network, 134 98th Avenue, Oakland, CA 94603.

**(Contact your librarian or a used bookstore
for locating out-of-print books).**

Glossary

ABRAHAM. Biblical character regarded as the patriarch of Christianity, Judaism and Islam.

ACHILLES HEEL. A serious weakness or vulnerable spot.

AL-AZHAR UNIVERSITY. In Cairo, a principal center of Arabic and Islamic study and the oldest continuous educational site in the Islamic world.

ANTI-SEMITE. Literally, one who is prejudiced against the descendants of the Biblical character Shem. These descendants include Arabs, Arameans, Babylonians, Carthaginians, Ethiopians, Hebrews, and Phoenicians. In America, the term is generally taken to mean only persons prejudiced against Jews (Hebrews).

ARAB. A Semite inhabiting Arabia, whose language and Islamic religion spread throughout the Middle East and northern Africa during the seventh century.

ASSASSIN. A member of a secret Islamic sect originating in the 11th century and dedicated to warfare by the means of killing leaders only. The sect is widely believed to have disappeared or to have been absorbed by the Ismaili sect, but no one knows for sure.

ASSASSINATION. The killing of a leader.

BARBARY COAST. The shore of the Mediterranean from the Atlantic to Egypt. The name is derived from the Berbers who inhabit the area.

BARBARY STATES. The Arab-Moslem states of the Barbary Coast until the mid-1800s when they were conquered by the Europeans.

BILL OF RIGHTS. The first ten amendments to the U.S. Constitution.

BLACK MARKET. Producing, buying or selling something against the wishes of the government. Example: Liquor was a black market product during America's "Prohibition Era."

CATHOLIC. Roman Catholic; a follower of the Church of Rome.

CBN. Chemical, biological and nuclear weapons, meant to kill thousands at a time. Also known as WMD, weapons of mass destruction.

CHAOSTAN. (see map, page 183) (pronunciation: Chaostan). A word coined by Richard Maybury, means the land of chaos. The area from the Arctic Ocean to the Indian Ocean and Poland to the Pacific, plus North Africa. This is the most important area that never developed legal systems based on the two fundamental laws that make civilization possible: (1) do all you have agreed to do and (2) do not encroach on other persons or their property. These laws are taught by all religions.

CHRISTIAN. A follower of Jesus Christ.

CHRISTIANITY. The collection of religions based on the teachings of Jesus Christ.

CONVENTIONAL WEAPONS. Knives, spears, bullets, napalm, high-explosives or any other weapon that does not fall into the category of CBN.

COLD WAR. The conflict between the U.S. and Soviet governments between 1945 and 1990.

COSSACKS. A fiercely Christian group from southern European Russia. Noted as cavalrymen, they were the "sword arm of the Czars," and the spearhead of attacks on Moslems.

CROAT. An inhabitant of Croatia. Most Croats are Roman Catholic.

CRUSADES. The wars launched by Europeans against Moslems during the Middle Ages.

CUSTOMS. Originally, the customary amount of goods (or money) stolen from merchandise crossing a border or checkpoint; today, the government agency that forcibly collects money for goods crossing a border or checkpoint.

DE FACTO. In fact, in reality. De facto power means actually exercising power though not legally or officially allowed to.

DEPRESSION. The correction period following an inflation. Usually includes a lot of business failures and unemployment.

DICTATOR. An absolute ruler; a tyrant or despot.

EASTERN ORTHODOX CHRISTIANITY. One of the three main branches of Christianity, the others being Roman Catholicism and Protestantism. The eastern Orthodox and Roman Catholic churches split in 1054 A.D. Orthodox churches include but are not limited to the Russian Orthodox, Greek Orthodox, Romanian Orthodox, Serbian Orthodox and Armenian Orthodox. Because of their geographic location, members of the Orthodox churches have an especially intense history of conflict with the Islamic world.

ECONOMICS. The study of the production and distribution of goods and services.

ETHNIC CLEANSING. A term coined in the Balkan wars of the 1990s, means the removal of a group from a geographic area by whatever means appears necessary including wholesale extermination.

EUROCENTRIC. A Europe-centered view of the world, said of Europhiles.

EUROPHILE. One who admires and feels loyalty to Europe.

FRANJ. During the Crusades the Arabic word for French. Today this word is still used in colloquial Arabic to mean Westerner; it is not a compliment.

FREEZE ASSETS. To enact legislation placing assets beyond the legal reach of their owners.

GULF OF SIDRA. A section of Mediterranean waters off Libya.

HUBRIS. Excessive pride, arrogance. The assumption that one knows what is best for others or has the right to impose one's will on others.

INFLATION. An increase in the amount of money. Causes the money to lose value, so prices rise.

INFRASTRUCTURE. An imprecise term generally meaning the basic facilities needed for the functioning of a community, such as roads, buildings, electrical lines, airports and bridges. Fixed assets.

IRAN. Persia.

IRAN-IRAQ WAR. The 1980-88 war between Iran and Iraq. Iraq attacked Iran, and was then given assistance by the White House and Kremlin.

IRAQ-KUWAIT WAR. The 1990-91 war between Saddam Hussein and George Bush.

ISAAC. Son of Abraham. Jews and Christians trace their descent from Isaac.

ISHMAEL. Son of Abraham. Moslems trace their descent from Ishmael.

ISLAM. Religion and political system founded by Mohammed. Opponent of the Christian West in the Thousand Year War. "Islam" means "submission" to God's law.

ISLAMIC WORLD. Nations with majority Moslem populations. Roughly the area from Morocco to Pakistan, plus much of Southeast Asia, and Kazakhstan to the Indian Ocean.

JESUS. The leader of the Christians, died around 29 A.D.

JEW. One who adheres to Judaism as a religion or culture.

JIHAD. Islamic term for holy war.

JUDAISM. The Jewish religion which traces its origin from Abraham.

KORAN. The holy book of the Moslems, contains the teachings of Mohammed.

KURDS. The pastoral and agricultural people who inhabit Kurdistan, a region of northern Iraq, eastern Turkey and Syria, and western Iran. Most Kurds are Sunni Moslem.

MACHIAVELLIAN. Exceedingly evil and deceptive in political matters. From the Italian political theorist Machiavelli whose book THE PRINCE (1513) describes the acquisition and maintenance of political power by a ruler who has no ethics.

MAHDI. The Guided One, a hero who will come from God to unite Moslems against their enemies.

MANTRA. A verbal formula repeated in prayer or meditation.

MIDDLE EAST. An imprecise term usually taken to mean the area from Egypt or Sudan to Afghanistan, but also often taken to mean the Arab-Moslem world.

MIDEAST. Middle East.

MOHAMMED. The leader of the Moslems who died in 632 A.D.

MOHAMMEDAN. Moslem.

MOOR. Moslem.

MOOSLIM. Moslem.

MORISCO. Moslem.

MOSES. The leading prophet of the Jews who died around 1200 B.C.

MOSLEMS. People who practice the Islamic religion. Most live in the enormous region stretching from Morocco to the Philippines, and from the equator to northern Kazakhstan.

MUSLIM. Moslem.

NATO. North Atlantic Treaty Organization. A military alliance of the U.S. and west European nations originally formed to counter the Soviet Union. Now that the Soviet Union has fallen apart, and NATO gives money and military training to Russia, NATO's purpose is undefined and may be evolving into an anti-Moslem alliance in the Thousand Year War.

NEPOTISM. Favoritism shown toward relatives.

NON-STATIST. One who opposes large, powerful governments and believes in liberty, free markets and international neutrality.

NORIEGA, MANUEL. Corrupt and brutal ruler of Panama in the 1980s, backed by the U.S. government until U.S. officials decided to launch a war to get rid of him in 1989.

ORTHODOX CHRISTIANITY. See Eastern Orthodox Christianity.

PALESTINE. The Holy Land. Was the site of the ancient kingdoms of Israel and Judah and today comprises Israel and parts of Jordan. The borders of Palestine have fluctuated but have generally included the territory lying between the southeastern Mediterranean coast, the Jordan and Dead Sea Valley, the Negev Desert, and the Litani River.

PALESTINIAN. An Arab inhabitant of Palestine.

PAPER TIGER. One who appears dangerous and powerful but is in fact timid and weak.

PERSIA. Iran.

PERSIAN. Of or relating to Persia. Persians (Iranians) are often lumped together with Arabs, but Persians are a separate group, and are ancient enemies of Arabs.

POLITICAL POWER. The privilege of using force on persons who have not harmed anyone. The privilege of backing one's decisions with violence or threats of violence. This privilege is what sets government apart from all other institutions.

RUSSIAN. Inhabitant of Russia. Russians are light-skinned slavs of Eastern Orthodox Christian heritage, and traditional enemies of Moslems.

SALADIN. Moslem leader who successfully led battles to throw Europeans out of the Holy Land during the 12th century. A role model for Islamic rebels today.

SARACEN. European term for Arab Moslems. The term meant "barbarian."

SAUDI ARABIA. The largest state on the Arabian peninsula, the home of Mecca and Medina, and the world's largest source of oil. A dictatorship ruled by the Saudi royal family who rose to power with the help of the British.

SEMITE. Descendant of Biblical character Shem; includes Arabs, Arameans, Babylonians, Carthaginians, Ethiopians, Hebrews, and Phoenicians.

SERB. Inhabitant of Serbia. Light-skinned Slavs with an Eastern Orthodox Christian heritage, Serbs are traditional enemies of Moslems, especially Turks, and allies of Russians and other Eastern Orthodox Christians. Serbs historically see themselves in the vanguard of the battle to save Europe from the Moslems.

SHIITE. A member of the Shia branch of Islam. Shiites regard Ali and his descendants as the legal successors to Mohammed. Shiites are ancient enemies of Sunnis.

STATIST. One who believes in a powerful, activist government that has the privilege of intervention in the economic and private lives of citizens and foreigners.

SUBJUGATE. To conquer. To make subservient or enslave.

SUNNI. A member of the Sunni branch of Islam. Sunnis accept the first four caliphs as legitimate successors of Mohammed, Most Moslems are Sunni. Sunnis and Shiites are ancient enemies.

SURROGATE. Substitute.

TAQIYYA. A doctrine of dispensation. Moslems are required to practice their faiths but when under duress are permitted by taqiyya to conceal and disguise their beliefs.

TERRORISM. An extremely vague, undefined term (one man's terrorist is another man's freedom fighter) that usually indicates someone who fights with weapons or tactics that are considered by the victims to be unfair. Highly useful in political propaganda, it accuses, tries and convicts a person with a single word. The word should not be used when precise thought is desired.

THOUSAND YEAR WAR. Term coined by Richard J. Maybury. The war between the Islamic world and the Europeans that began during the Middle Ages with the Crusades.

TRIPOLI. City in Libya. Also, the occasional name of the city of Tarabulous in Lebanon.

TURK. An inhabitant of Turkey. Turks originated in the Altai Mountains of east Asia, and during the Middle Ages migrated west to conquer Turkey and create the Ottoman Empire. Turkic civilization stretches from the Balkans to the Pacific.

UNITED NATIONS. An organization composed of most of the governments of the world, founded in 1945 supposedly to promote peace, security, and economic progress. The UN is slowly evolving into a world government.

WEST, THE. The Islamic world's term for the U.S. and Europe. The Christian world.

ZIONISM. A political movement intended to create a Jewish state.

About
Richard J. Maybury
"Uncle Eric"

Richard J. Maybury, also known as "Uncle Eric," is the former Global Affairs editor of Moneyworld, and widely regarded as one of the top free-market writers in America. His articles have appeared in the Wall Street Journal, USA Today and other major publications.

He's been a consultant to business firms in the U.S. and Europe. He is president of Henry-Madison Research.

His books have been endorsed by top business leaders including former U.S. Treasury Secretary William Simon, and he has been interviewed on more than 200 radio and TV shows across America.

He is the author of the "Uncle Eric" series of books and writes an investment newsletter.

He's been around the world, and visited 47 states and 32 countries.

He is a teacher for all ages.

Index

Henry-Madison Research

Richard Maybury is president of Henry-Madison Research. He writes an investment newsletter about stocks, geopolitics, economics, bonds, currencies, real estate, interest rates, precious metals and more. Much analysis is based on the connection between law and economics. Mr. Maybury gives special attention to events in the former USSR and Mideast, as well as in the U.S.

For a sample pack including the most recent issue of Richard Maybury's EARLY WARNING REPORT newsletter, plus a detailed map of Chaostan and the six-page special report CHAOSTAN, THE FULL STORY — a $25.00 value — send $10.00 to Henry Madison Research, Dept. 292, Box 84908, Phoenix, AZ 85071.

I have ever deemed it fundamental for the United States never to take active part in the quarrels of Europe. Their political interests are entirely distinct from ours. Their mutual jealousies, their balance of power, their complicated alliances, their forms and principles of government, are all foreign to us. They are nations of eternal war."

— Thomas Jefferson, 1823

.."a passionate attachment of one nation for another produces a variety of evils. Sympathy for the favorite nation, facilitating the illusion of an imaginary common interest in cases where no real common interest exists, and infusing into one the enmities of the other, betrays the former into a participation in the quarrels and wars of the latter, without adequate inducement or justification. It leads also to concession to the favorite nation of privileges denied to others, which is apt doubly to injure the nation making the concessions; by unnecessarily parting with what ought to have been retained; and by exciting jealousy, ill-will and a disposition to retaliate, in the parties from whom equal privileges are withheld. And it gives to ambitious, corrupted or deluded citizens (who devote themselves to the favorite nation) facility to betray, or sacrifice the interests of their own country, without odium, sometimes even with popularity .... Against the insidious wiles of foreign influence, (I conjure you to believe me fellow-citizen) the jealousy of a free people ought to be constantly awake."

— George Washington
FAREWELL ADDRESS, 1796

Bluestocking Press

Besides being the publisher of Richard J. Maybury's "Uncle Eric" books, Bluestocking Press also publishes a catalog, for ages preK through adult, which specializes in American history, economics, law, and entrepreneurship.

History selections include: fiction, nonfiction, primary source material, historical documents, facsimile newspapers, historical music, toy-making kits, and more.

At the time of this writing, the Bluestocking Press Catalog includes approximately 800 items. The catalog is free with your book order (see next page). Otherwise, for immediate first class shipping of the catalog please remit:

U.S. addresses: $3.00.

Foreign addresses: $3.00 surface shipping.
or $5.00 air shipping.

Make checks or money orders payable in U.S. funds to Bluestocking Press.

Bluestocking Press
P.O. Box 1014 • Dept. TYW • Placerville • CA • 95667 • USA

Phone orders: 530-621-1123; 800-959-8586
FAX: 530-642-9222

(MC, Visa and American Express orders accepted)

Bluestocking Press

"Uncle Eric" Books by Richard J. Maybury

UNCLE ERIC TALKS ABOUT PERSONAL, CAREER & FINANCIAL SECURITY. . . . . $ 7.95

WHATEVER HAPPENED TO PENNY CANDY? . . . .$ 9.95

WHATEVER HAPPENED TO JUSTICE? $14.95

ARE YOU LIBERAL? CONSERVATIVE? OR CONFUSED? . . . . $ 9.95

ANCIENT ROME: HOW IT AFFECTS YOU TODAY . . . . $ 8.95

EVALUATING BOOKS: WHAT WOULD THOMAS JEFFERSON THINK ABOUT THIS? . . . $ 8.95

THE MONEY MYSTERY . . . . $ 8.95

THE CLIPPER SHIP STRATEGY $15.95

THE THOUSAND YEAR WAR IN THE MIDEAST: HOW IT AFFECTS YOU TODAY $17.95

Uncle Eric's Model (SAVE! Includes nine books above) $93.00

Bluestocking Guides by Jane A. Williams

BLUESTOCKING GUIDE: ECONOMICS—BASED ON RICHARD J. MAYBURY'S BOOK WHAT-
EVER HAPPENED TO PENNY CANDY. Includes: 1) chapter-by-chapter comprehension
questions and answers for WHATEVER HAPPENED TO PENNY CANDY, 2) activities, 3)
articles that expand on the concepts presented in WHATEVER HAPPENED TO PENNY
CANDY, 4) movies that contain good economic history, 5) a final exam and 6) **an
economic timetable** (researched and compiled with the help of Richard J.
Maybury) 124 pgs, 8 1/2" x 11" $12.95

BLUESTOCKING GUIDE: ANCIENT ROME—BASED ON RICHARD J. MAYBURY'S BOOK
ANCIENT ROME: HOW IT AFFECTS YOU TODAY . . . . query for price

Study Guides are forthcoming for other "Uncle Eric" books. Query publisher.

Related Bluestocking Press Titles

JONATHAN MAYHEW'S SERMON $4.95

Prices subject to change without notice—confirm price with publisher
before ordering. Phone 530-621-1123 • 800-959-8586 • Fax 530-642-9222

Order information: Order any of the above from Bluestocking Press (see address
below). Payable in U.S. funds. Add shipping/handling as follows: First book, add
$3.00 (book rate shipping) or $4.00 (foreign orders, surface shipping); each
additional book: add $1.00. California residents add sales tax.

The Bluestocking Press Catalog, for ages preK through adult, specializes in
American history, economics, law, and entrepreneurship. History selections
include: fiction, nonfiction, primary source material, historical documents,
facsimile newspapers, historical music, toy-making kits, and more. Catalog free
with book order. Otherwise for immediate first class shipping of the catalog please
remit: U.S. addresses: $3.00. Foreign addresses: $3.00 surface shipping or $5.00
·ᵣ shipping. Payable in U.S. funds to Bluestocking Press.

Bluestocking Press
ᵧx 1014 • Dept. TYW • Placerville • CA • 95667 • USA
ders: 530-621-1123; 800-959-8586 (for MC / Visa orders)
FAX: 530-642-9222